studio
stories

Janis Ian with saxophonist Artie Kaplan, Mira Sound, 1967.

studio
stories

DAVID SIMONS

HOW THE GREAT NEW YORK RECORDS WERE MADE: FROM MILES TO MADONNA. SINATRA TO THE RAMONES

studio stories
DAVID SIMONS

A BACKBEAT BOOK
First edition 2004
Published by Backbeat Books
600 Harrison Street
San Francisco, CA 94107, US
www.backbeatbooks.com

An imprint of The Music Player Network, United Entertainment Media Inc.

Published for Backbeat Books by Outline Press Ltd,
2A Union Court, 20-22 Union Road, London SW4 6JP, England
www.backbeatuk.com

ISBN 0-87930-817-6

For Frank Laico

EDITOR John Morrish
EDITORIAL DIRECTOR Tony Bacon
ART DIRECTOR Nigel Osborne
DESIGN Paul Cooper Design

Printed by Colorprint (Hong Kong)

04 05 06 07 08 5 4 3 2 1

contents

The vintage map on the right, created by Hermann Bollmann, shows the principal area in New York City for recording studios in the early 1960s. Each highlighted number on the map indicates the location of a studio featured in this book and detailed in the list below, which also gives a brief selection of some of the hits and other key records made at the various studios. After that is a list of the other major studios featured in the book that are located beyond the area of the map.

1. A&R STUDIO 1
112 W. 48th St.
'SOUL BOSSA NOVA' Quincy Jones 1962
'THE GIRL FROM IPANEMA'
   Stan Getz / Astrud Gilberto 1964
'I THANK THE LORD FOR THE NIGHT TIME'
   Neil Diamond 1967
'I DIG ROCK AND ROLL MUSIC'
   Peter Paul & Mary 1967
'BROWN EYED GIRL' Van Morrison 1967
'DOMINO' Van Morrison 1970

2. MIRA SOUND
145 W. 47th St.
'HEY GIRL' Freddie Scott 1963
'REMEMBER (WALKIN' IN THE SAND)'
   The Shangri-Las 1964
'SOCIETY'S CHILD' Janis Ian 1967

3. ASSOCIATED SOUND STUDIOS
723 7th Ave.
'MY BOYFRIEND'S BACK' The Angels 1963
'HANG ON SLOOPY' The McCoys 1965

4. DICK CHARLES STUDIO
729 7th Ave.
'CHERRY, CHERRY' Neil Diamond 1973

5. STEI-PHILIPS STUDIOS 7th Ave.
'SHERRY' The 4 Seasons 1962

6. COLUMBIA STUDIO A
799 7th Ave.
'HOMEWARD BOUND'
   Simon & Garfunkel 1966
'SUMMER IN THE CITY'
   Lovin' Spoonful 1966
A&R Studio 2 799 7th Ave.
'THE WEIGHT' The Band 1968
'A SIMPLE TWIST OF FATE' Bob Dylan 1975

7. WORLD UNITED STUDIOS
1595 Broadway
'WALK AWAY RENEE' Left Banke 1966

8. BRILL BUILDING 1619 Broadway
THE MUSIC INDUSTRY'S SONGWRITING
   'FACTORY'.

9. ALLEGRO SOUND (also Scepter, Aldon) 1650 Broadway
'RAG DOLL' The 4 Seasons 1964
'YOUNGER GIRL' The Critters 1966

'SOCK IT TO ME BABY' Mitch Ryder &
   The Detroit Wheels 1967
'MONY, MONY'
   Tommy James & the Shondells 1968

10. BELL SOUND (later Hit Factory) 237 W. 54th St.
'WALK ON BY' Dionne Warwick 1964
'RAINDROPS KEEP FALLING ON MY HEAD'
   B.J. Thomas 1969
'ROCK AND ROLL ALL NITE' Kiss 1975

11. ATLANTIC STUDIO 1 (later A-1)
234 W. 56th St.
'SHAKE, RATTLE & ROLL'
   Big Joe Turner 1954

12. ATLANTIC STUDIO 3
11 W. 60th St.
'BABY I LOVE YOU' Aretha Franklin 1967
'SUNSHINE OF YOUR LOVE' Cream 1968

13. ATLANTIC STUDIO 2
156 W. 57th St.
'CHARLIE BROWN' The Coasters 1959

14. COLUMBIA STUDIO B
49 E. 52nd St.
'PIECE OF MY HEART' Big Brother &
   the Holding Company 1968
'THE ONLY LIVING BOY IN NEW YORK'
   Simon & Garfunkel 1970

15. CENTURY SOUND
135 W. 52nd St.
'SWEET CAROLINE' Neil Diamond 1969

16. TALENTMASTERS RECORDING STUDIO 126 W. 42nd St.
'IT'S A MAN'S, MAN'S, MAN'S WORLD'
   James Brown 1966
'COOL JERK' The Capitols 1966
'I CAN SEE FOR MILES' The Who 1967

BEYOND THE MAP...

BELTONE STUDIOS 33rd St.
'I MET HIM ON A SUNDAY'
   The Shirelles 1958

COLUMBIA 30TH STREET
207 E. 30th St.

'TAKE FIVE' Dave Brubeck 1961
'I LEFT MY HEART IN SAN FRANCISCO'
   Tony Bennett 1962
'SING A SIMPLE SONG'
   Sly & the Family Stone 1969
'THEME FROM NEW YORK, NEW YORK'
   Frank Sinatra 1980

ELECTRIC LADY STUDIOS
52 W. 8th St.
'SUPERSTITION' Stevie Wonder 1972
'FAME' David Bowie 1975
'SAY IT AIN'T SO' Weezer 1995

JUGGY SOUND W. 54th St.
'RAMBLE ON' Led Zeppelin 1969

MEDIASOUND 311 W. 57th St.
'HOLLYWOOD SWINGING'
   Kool & the Gang 1974
'ROCKAWAY BEACH' The Ramones 1977

POWER STATION (later Avatar)
441 W. 53rd St.
'HUNGRY HEART' Bruce Springsteen 1980
'LET'S DANCE' David Bowie 1983
'LIKE A VIRGIN' Madonna 1984

PYTHIAN TEMPLE 135 W. 70th St.
'ROCK AROUND THE CLOCK' Bill Haley &
   his Comets 1954

RCA STUDIO A AND B
155 East 24th St.
'YOUR FEET'S TOO BIG' (A) Fats Waller 1939
'DON'T BE CRUEL' (A) Elvis Presley 1956
'A LITTLE BIT ME, A LITTLE BIT YOU'
   (B) The Monkees 1967

RCA WEBSTER HALL 125 11th St.
'BANANA BOAT (DAY-O)'
   Harry Belafonte 1957
'SAMBALERO' Stan Getz, Luiz Bonfa 1963

RECORD PLANT 321 W. 44th St.
'SCHOOL'S OUT' Alice Cooper 1972
'(JUST LIKE) STARTING OVER'
   John Lennon 1980

SUNDRAGON STUDIO (later Streetlight) 20th St.
'BLITZKRIEG BOP' The Ramones 1976
'PSYCHO KILLER' Talking Heads 1977

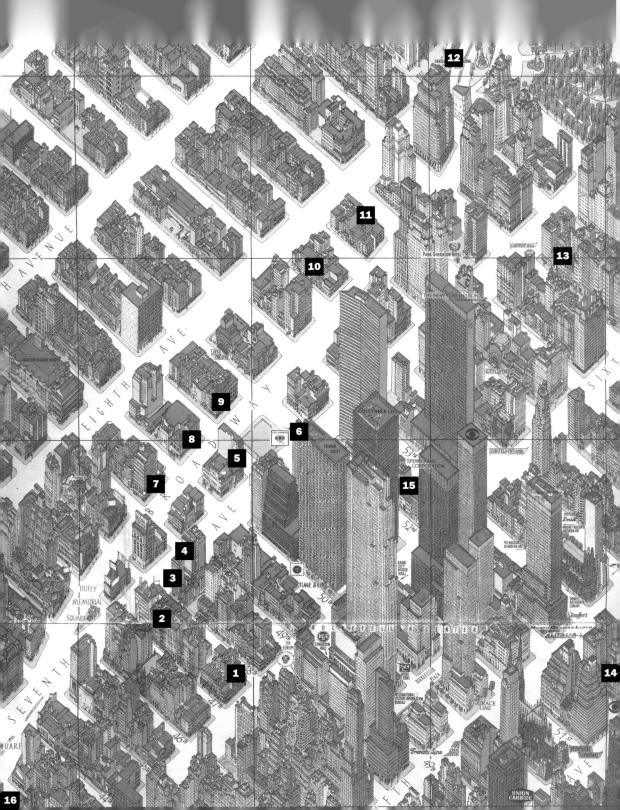

new york recording
now – and then

The bright red awnings of Maxie's Delicatessen add color to the otherwise drab exterior of 723 7th Avenue, an ancient 12-story structure that has played a part in creating some of the most popular sounds made in the city of New York.

Since 1978, the building, at the corner of West 48th Street, has been home to Quad Recording Studios, owned by veteran engineer Lou Gonzalez. Its client list includes modern hitmakers like Alicia Keys, Destiny's Child and Coldplay. Quad's predecessor, Associated Sound, was a favorite hangout for 1960s songwriters like Barry Mann and Cynthia Weil, and the birthplace of 'My Boyfriend's Back' and other hits of the girl-group era.

The interior of 723 7th is remarkably well preserved. Riding up the old-style elevator, one can easily imagine producer Jeff Barry on his way to a sixth-floor session, or Carole King heading back to her Broadway cubicle to finish off 'Hey Girl' with husband Gerry Goffin.

Gonzalez, who got his start turning the dials at Bob Goldman's Mira Sound Studios in the late 1960s, has never completely shed his sense of tradition: a fleet of Studer tape machines and other relics of the past has been seamlessly integrated into each of Quad's state-of-the-art recording rooms. Still, Quad's beautifully appointed studios are a reminder of just how much the business of making music has changed over the years. Sleek, automated consoles have long since replaced the funky old mixing desks of yesteryear. Where artists once labored to get the job done in two hours using three tracks, Quad's visitors are afforded a virtually endless supply of work space.

The same technology that transformed full-service studios like Quad over the past decade also lit a fire under the home-studio market. Today, even the most basic do-it-yourself machine offers at least eight recording tracks (four more than the Beatles had) and an array of built-in effects, giving musicians the freedom to work on new ideas on the spot rather than wait to book studio time or assemble a crew of players. Its impact on the record industry has been considerable.

"Nearly one-third of the hits I've done have originated in the home or home-type studio," notes Dave 'Hard Drive' Pensado, who helped deliver Pink's 2001 classic *M!ssundaztood* album.

"In many ways there are a lot of things the home guys do that are in fact better than the recordings that come from a big facility. That's because, in general, the creativity that emerges from a home studio almost always surpasses that of an expensive studio. Never mind the sound quality – personally, I'd rather start with the kind of feeling and emotion you get on a homemade record like Pink's. That's the main thing."

For those who believe that an Internet-based musical revolution is at hand, the prospect of a 16-track in every garage is certainly good news. But there's a flip side to all this digital democracy. As sophisticated machinery like ProTools becomes more affordable, even professional artists are now minimizing their trips to the studio. The increasingly popular practice of shuttling tracks back and forth between living room and control room means that, now more than ever, records are being produced bit by bit, rather than in one large gulp, as was once the norm. Great for the bottom line, perhaps – but not always the best thing for the listener.

"When you have excellent players all working together at once, there is usually some friendly competition. People tend to perform to the best of their abilities," notes Matt Wallace, producer for Maroon 5, Faith No More and Paul Westerberg. "The interaction sparks additional excitement, thereby creating a more lively track. It plays a large part in the overall warmth and spirit of the recording. That's what's at stake when you go it alone."

Moreover, the ability to fine-tune every element of the recorded work – combined with the more leisurely approach to recording that is itself a byproduct of the digital age – has all but removed the chance for anything haphazard or accidental from sneaking onto the finished product.

"People now have the wherewithal to make really perfect-sounding records," says Wallace. "But from my experience, as the quality of the recording gets better, the quality of the musicianship very often suffers. The result is a safer, homogenized product." Josh Freese, a top session drummer who has worked for Evanescence, Avril Lavigne and the Offspring adds, "Let's face it – when you've got Pro Tools, there's no need for those pesky chops."

THE WAY IT WAS

Looking down on to 7th Avenue from Quad's lounge area, I tried to visualize the music scene as it once was. Directly below stood the buildings that once controlled the world's airwaves. To see how close these now-defunct studios were to one another is to understand the creativity and spontaneity of the New York recording environment during the 1950s and 1960s. (See the 1962 map on page 7.) A few feet to the right sits 729 7th, formerly Dick Charles Studio, where Neil Diamond cut 'Cherry, Cherry' one summer's afternoon in 1966. Down 48th Street is the spot where Phil Ramone made history with his first A&R Studio.

Dead ahead at 1619 Broadway is the Brill Building. Right next door is 1650 Broadway, where the former home of Don Kirshner's Aldon Music was upstairs, while downstairs was Allegro Sound Studio, birthplace to innumerable Tommy James hits.

The corner of 51st and 7th is Stei-Philips Studios, where The 4 Seasons scored first with 'Sherry,' directly across the street from CBS's 799 7th Avenue studios, where Barbara Streisand recorded her Columbia debut.

Only a handful of the studios covered in this book are still with us today. Oversized rooms like the Pythian Temple and Columbia's famed 30th Street Studio have been transformed into apartment buildings. Mediasound Studio and Webster Hall are now nightclubs. On West 47th, a Euro-styled hotel marks the spot where Shadow Morton cut his historic sides with The Shangri-Las and Janis Ian.

The forces that compelled the flight from the cities to the suburbs during the 1960s and 1970s – noisy traffic, cranky neighbors, and, most of all, booming rents – brought to an end New York's era of recording dominance. In the years that followed, Los Angeles gained its share of producer and engineer defectors, as did Miami, Nashville and various other locales around the world.

Times have changed. Corporations that once paid to dismantle rock'n'roll now shell out millions for the privilege of using a classic-rock excerpt in an ad campaign. As the business of selling rock has become bigger and bigger, the business of making rock has become increasingly streamlined, setting the stage for the studio as we now know it: an immaculate, automated environment complete with handsome floors and paneling, soft lighting, and – most important – a separate space for every player and sound source. Today, a select few equipment manufacturers supply the majority of the world's professional studios. Gone are the hand-made consoles, echo chambers and other specialized items that once gave a studio its unique sound.

> "A FIFTIES JAZZ RECORD CAN BE THE CLOSEST THING WE HAVE TO BEING IN THE ROOM WITHOUT ACTUALLY BEING IN THE ROOM."

"Many studios have become what is known in economics as 'an undifferentiated product,'" says Walter Sear, owner of Sear Sound, the oldest operating studio in Manhattan. "One sack of rice is the same as the next."

And yet classic recording techniques have not been completely forgotten. During the 1990s, mixers like Butch Vig, Brendan O'Brien, Don Smith, Jim Scott, Neill King, and Niko Bolas launched a mini backlash, utilizing old-school techniques and technology in an effort to put some of the dynamics back into the recording environment. Despite the trend away from large, live rooms, places like New York's Right Track – whose 38th Street location boasts a 4,600 square foot orchestral studio reminiscent of old-school facilities like CBS and RCA – proves that the age of ambience is far from over. "When you're recording the music live in a room with a lot of space – that's the only time that you can really hear the make-up of the studio," says Gonzalez. "And that's so important."

Bringing yesterday's methods into today's workplace is a challenge that producers like Gonzalez and Wallace accept on a daily basis. "One of my favorite sessions was working with Paul Westerberg on *14 Songs*, some of which was done at RPM Studios here in New York," says Wallace. "We'd track the songs live with Paul on electric guitar, with the idea of getting the master take within two or three tries. A perfectly executed, no mistake take? No way – but what you do get is a track that's steeped in spirit. Which I'll take any day of the week."

"By combining modern technology with the traditional craft of recording, good old equipment and good new equipment – and using musicality and good taste – good work is still being done," notes Sear. "Just not often enough."

REAL ROOMS AND A BURST OF TECHNOLOGY

Over the course of history, every so often we've managed to undo something that is already a proven success. Take the record business. By 1980, digital recording technology had emerged, bringing with it machinery and methods that were considered revolutionary compared to those of yesteryear. Yet many of the records produced during that time now sound thin and dated. "But then you put on a 1950s jazz record," remarks producer Jon Brion, "and it's still the closest thing we have to being in the room without actually being in the room. It's incredible. How did we lose all that technology?"

Make no mistake: Sonny Rollins' *Saxophone Colossus*, Miles Davis's *Kind of Blue*, Dave Brubeck's *Time Out*, or any of the unsurpassed masters from New York's 'golden era' of sound would not have been possible without the burst of technology that had, just a few years earlier, taken the business from wax to multiple tracks. But improved fidelity was just one part of the formula; the main ingredient was the room itself.

When housing a large group of players was a priority, record labels typically used existing structures for studio space, rather than erecting dedicated (and, as has often been the case in the modern era, sterile) facilities from scratch. In the city of New York, between the years 1945 and 1960, the best recording studios were fashioned out of old hotels, churches, electric plants, or simply abandoned office space; practically any kind of building was fair game. Studio owners at that time had one thing in common: a willingness to let the original composition of the structure remain a part of the recording environment. Thus, old, creaky wood floorboards were left unvarnished and unwashed;

dusty curtains hung in place for years; cement storage rooms were used to supply a live echo effect. Such artifacts contributed to the overall sound of each studio – and are the reason why the discerning listener can actually distinguish one room from another today.

"Those studios had what I like to call a 'fingerprint' sound," says veteran studio man Jimmy Johnson, producer for Wilson Pickett, Aretha Franklin and others. "The kind of places where you hear a record on the radio today and know immediately where it was cut. That's what made them so special."

As it so happens, some of the very best rooms in Manhattan had room to spare – which wasn't a luxury, but a necessity. Before multi-track recording technology made it possible for one or two players to sound like a roomful, a roomful of players was required. This was an era of cheap rents and low utilities; when it came to securing studio space, in some instances, the sky was the limit. Nowhere was that more evident than at Columbia's 30th Street Studio, a cavernous converted Armenian church that boasted 100-foot ceilings and floor space. Others, like Webster Hall and the Pythian Temple, helped maintain the bigger-is-better philosophy.

As anyone knows who has ever worked inside a half-empty auditorium, there's a fine line between making music and making unintelligible garbage when the space is too vast. Which is why the subtle tones that define Davis's *Kind of Blue* and Brubeck's *Time Out* – recorded within weeks of each other at the 30th Street Studio in 1959 – seem to defy the laws of physics. And yet, such wonders of nature occurred again and again at 30th Street, as well as in many other studios around the island of Manhattan.

Harnessing the enormous ambience of those rooms was not for the faint of heart. But in those heady times, the early 1950s, there emerged a select group of studio craftsmen whose ability to capture on tape the excitement of a live performance within a large studio setting – using few gadgets but endless ingenuity – made them the acknowledged masters of their trade. The names of these great audio engineers seldom appeared on album jackets in the 1950s and 1960s. Many have long since retired and are now living simple lives far removed from the fanfare of the music industry. Yet literally thousands of the world's most pivotal recordings bear their stamp.

ALL TOGETHER NOW

Improved technology and an optimal studio environment helped foster the tremendous outpouring of music during the 1950s and 1960s – but another important piece of the puzzle was the manner in which the music was recorded. While conducting the research for this book, I interviewed dozens of producers and engineers, responsible for most of the classic records discussed here. By the mid 1960s, lack of tracks was no longer an issue; most studios had either four- or eight-track tape machines at their disposal. Yet when they were asked how many tracks they employed at their hit-making peak, their answer was almost invariably the same: "We cut them totally live."

Throughout New York and the studio world at large, getting the goods on tape all at once had long been the accepted means of record making. The arrival of the multi-track recorder – introduced during the early 1950s, but regarded with suspicion by many within the industry – made it possible for the first time for artists to record in sections, rather than as a live ensemble as was required with mono or two-track machines. Nevertheless, live recording remained standard operating procedure in the studio as late as the end of the 1960s; Cream's *Disraeli Gears*, Van Morrison's *Moondance* and many other landmark albums from the time were mainly recorded without overdubs, despite having eight-track machines on the premises.

Recording vocals and instruments simultaneously may seem an awesome undertaking in the modern era. But 35 years ago, packed touring schedules and incessant demand for product (upwards of three albums a year) turned most recording artists into tight, thoroughly accomplished musicians. Though the Beatles would usher in the era of multi-track mania, with the likes of *Revolver* and *Sgt. Pepper's Lonely Hearts Club Band* (recorded on four-track, no less), the collaborative spirit that was a by-product of live tracking sessions was considered an essential element of a hit recording. As Ken Townsend, a former Beatles recording technician, observed, "There's a certain kind of spontaneity that occurs when you aren't multi-tracking everything. The Beatles' first few years proved that."

As the number of tracks rose during the 1970s, a concern with perfection gradually crept into the record-making process. Chris Huston, studio designer and noted producer-engineer for Van Morrison, James Brown, The Who and many others, remembers the turning point vividly. "Even when we had eight-track, sessions were still being done live," says Huston. "But by the early 1970s we had 16 tracks – which suddenly gave us the ability to put all the instruments on separate tracks. Initially it didn't work, because there was too much bleed between the instruments, the result of studios being designed to actually enhance the concept of live performance.

"So, in a further attempt to really isolate the instruments, in order to take full advantage of the 16-track technology, they started to deaden the studios. I mean, how stupid! The idea was that, with that many tracks, you could really control things, you could create something by having the ability to isolate and replace entire sections of a song. That immediately became apparent to those in the recording industry.

"And in order to pull it off, you had to also re-think the way the studio was constructed – because up until that point, you didn't have the wherewithal to really hone those parts individually. So in turn they began this new studio prototype: one where leakage could be maintained, if not completely eliminated. It was a tremendous change in the method of modern recording up to that point. And it turned everything on its tail."

To many listeners, the pristine fidelity that became the mid-1970s recording model was considered breathtaking; to others, the neurotic attention to detail made for a contrived, soulless product, especially in juxtaposition to the records that once defined the medium of pop radio. Records produced within a smaller, drier recording environment weren't nearly as vital-sounding, audio enthusiasts claimed, and for one good reason. As studios became smaller, artists were less likely to collaborate or perform live with a large group of players, for the simple reason that you couldn't always fit everyone in the room at the same time. An increasing number of artists and producers began to assemble their music in solitude, overdubbing parts one by one or using samples and processed sounds to create a backing track.

"Making records used to be like painting," remarked noted Columbia engineer Frank Laico. "Then it turned into assembling."

As the revamped studios went up, the old facilities that marked the recording industry's heyday gradually began to tumble. Accountants blamed economics; bigger studios required a bigger operating budget, and the smaller combos of the rock era required considerably less space than the largest rooms afforded. Advanced multi-track technology eliminated the need for live studio performance; the sequencers, samplers, drum machines and other products of the newly arrived digital era further reduced the space requirement by making it possible to record direct from the source with only marginal use of microphones. Theoretically, records could now be assembled in a room the size of a closet. Furthermore, the spirit of invention that informed the early years of pop recording was weakened – if not permanently displaced – by a succession of automated devices that transformed the art of creating recording effects into a matter of pushing buttons. Experimentation foundered.

From a business and space-saving standpoint, the new direction made perfect sense, but the era of 'recording the room' was now doomed to extinction.

"This may sound old fashioned, but the problem with a lot of recorded music these days is that there just isn't that kind of warmth," says Richard Lush, once a recording engineer for the Beatles and now senior engineer at 301 Studios in Sydney, Australia. "When something comes on that's live or has a bit of vibe to it, people's ears always prick up. That's what's happening when you listen to those period recordings. You can hear the drums going all over the vocal mic; there are things like limiters going on and off; as soon as the music stops the drums come up. All of those things are going on when you've got something happening live. It just adds to the excitement of it all. That kind of feeling is very hard to create if you're doing it layer by layer."

Particularly during the 1950s and 1960s, a large number of Big Apple bands weren't bands at all, but a tight-knit group of session players, who would turn up for work at facilities such as Mira Sound, Bell Sound or Columbia's 799 7th Avenue studio each morning, lunch pail in one hand and guitar case in the other, ready to take on the Flavor of the Week. Some worked for a prominent 'house band,' a musical collective that gave a studio its identifiable sound. The emergence of the self-contained performing group – led by the Beatles and their British peers – began an irreversible trend away from such backing ensembles; the brick-by-brick multitrack method sealed the deal, and transformed the business of music making into virtually a one-man show. The result: collaboration and creative input became less frequent.

There were other side effects as well:

- **Soundalikes.** As studios lost their 'fingerprint' sounds, entire genres lost their identity. For instance, today's country music bears little resemblance in sound and style to the music of old (and is, in fact, now largely marketed as pop music).
- **Ruling radio.** Musical homogenization helped foster a business climate that favored consolidation and monopolization of the airwaves; as ownership shrinks, stations lose their personality and local flavor.
- **The fading of live music.** Coincidentally or not, the decline in live performance as a studio component was paralleled by an overall reduction in live music as a social entity. Large ballrooms and nightclubs closed and performing musicians had far fewer outlets.

Despite the quantum leap in pro-recording technology, the world continues to embrace the sounds of yesteryear: 'classic' tracks recorded on 'obsolete' equipment, some 30-40 years ago. In order to understand our place in music history, we need to first understand why so many of the world's best-sounding records were the product of crusty old buildings that weren't even designed to be a recording studio in the first place.

What follows is an account of some of the most memorable moments in New York's recording history, as seen through the eyes (and ears) of the many producers, engineers, songwriters and recording artists who helped make them happen. While many of the names that appear within these pages will be familiar to even the most casual music fan, there are just as many whose accomplishments remain criminally under-appreciated.

The years 1950 to 1980 represent one of the most explosive periods in cultural history. And yet this fascinating era didn't just happen, it was the product of numerous ingredients: artists performing live in a large, vibrant recording space; producers and engineers spontaneously creating new effects and techniques; composers writing and re-writing parts on demand in the studio; session players crafting intros, riffs and arrangements, un-coached; and, most importantly, recording studios that had life, character, and an individual, easily identifiable sound that you can still hear on the radio today.

THE SOUND OF NEW YORK

For decades, recording studios reflected the unique vibrations of the regions they inhabited. The soul kitchens of Memphis and Muscle Shoals reverberated with the southern hybrid of country and R&B; the boogie-woogie and barrelhouse piano riffs emerging from Cosimo Mattasa's New Orleans studio gave listeners an earful of the energy coming off the streets outside.

In the city of New York, the convergence of cultures created a musical palate unlike any in the world. From the vaudeville era came young Jewish composers like brothers George and Ira Gershwin, Jerome Kern, and Irving Berlin. All were leaders of the formidable songwriting community on New York's East 14th Street, which came to be known as 'Tin Pan Alley.' Years later, the action would move uptown to a series of offices in and around the Brill Building at 1619 Broadway, where a new generation of tunesmiths – from Gerry Goffin and Carole King to Burt Bacharach and Hal David – turned out hundreds of pop hits ranging from 'Will You Love Me Tomorrow' and 'Twist and Shout' to 'Baby It's You' and 'Walk on By.'

Though jazz had its roots in New Orleans and Memphis, by the 1930s its centre was the thriving nightclub scene uptown in Harlem, a wellspring of musical activity that attracted an array of new talent. At venues like the Cotton Club, the Shalamar, and the Paradise, jazz dignitaries such as the great Duke Ellington, Fats Waller, Billie Holiday and Ella Fitzgerald worked the crowds seven nights a week. In subsequent years, the action spilled over into Manhattan's mid-town region, particularly at the Five Spot and the famed Birdland nightclub, named for legendary sax man Charlie 'Yardbird' Parker.

The recording technology of the 1930s and 1940s had come a long way since the early years of sound reproduction, when musicians would gather around a large funnel-shaped horn and create acoustic vibrations that formed grooves on a turning cylinder. In the mid 1920s, the microphone ushered in the era of electrical recording; for the first time, vocalists were afforded the luxury of singing at sub-operatic levels, rather than bellowing to be heard over an orchestra. The impact of the new apparatus was swift and dramatic; almost overnight, 'intimate' pop singing as a recording technique was born.

Leading the trend was an unlikely hero: singer Bing Crosby. "The condenser microphone was much more friendly to baritones than to tenors," notes Gary Giddins, *Village Voice* columnist and author of *Bing Crosby: A Pocketful of Dreams*, "because the baritone is a voice that gets its power in nuance and subtlety in the middle and lower range. Bing had that kind of voice, and the microphone allowed the intimacy of those nuances to be projected. ... Bing also understood the microphone, and that electricity paradoxically makes music more rather than less human; because you don't have to shout, you don't have to ring the rafters, you can now sing in a normal tone of voice.

"And if you combine his style – which is intimate in part because he actually interpreted the meaning of the lyrics, something that virtually no one was doing then – if you combine that with the microphone, you get a certain erotic undercurrent in popular music that didn't exist before, outside of the blues and certain regional kinds of music."

> "THE MICROPHONE'S IMPACT WAS SWIFT AND DRAMATIC – ALMOST OVERNIGHT, INTIMATE POP SINGING AS A TECHNIQUE WAS BORN."

Despite the various enhancements, record making from the time was hardly a leisurely operation. Until the late 1940s, performances were electronically 'printed' onto a rotating wax disc – known as the 'master' – from which copies could later be 'cut.' Once a recording began, there was no turning back; one small goof and the disc would be ruined and the performers forced to start from scratch. Mistakes were simply not an option; getting it right the first time was paramount.

Meanwhile, an entirely new subset of sounds was fast becoming part of New York's musical make-up. During the early 1950s, R&B, a stripped-down version of jump blues, gained favor on the back of artists such as Ruth Brown and The Coasters. By the middle of the decade, the street appeal of R&B would touch off yet another explosion: rock'n'roll.

Along with R&B came the short-lived but undeniably essential doo-wop genre. A distillation of vocal jazz and blues within a pop-song format, doo-wop was popularized by teenaged a cappella groups, who performed in the churches and on the street corners of New York and its boroughs. By the beginning of the 1960s, the reign of groups like The Cadillacs, The Capris, and The Coasters had ended, but their vocal style would inspire artists for years to come.

By that time, improvements in sound recording had already revolutionized the music business, thanks in no small part to the research of Lieutenant Jack Mullin, an electronics engineer who stumbled upon the German 'magnetophon' (a recording device that used magnetic tape spooled between a pair of reels) while stationed in Europe at the end of World War II. Mullin shipped several of the machines back to the States, piece by piece. Later, Mullin and partner Bill Palmer stunned executives of NBC with a demonstration of the new tape-based device. In 1947, Bing Crosby himself became the first popular artist to move from wax disc to magnetic-tape recording, using Mullin's Magnetophon. When the Ampex Corporation unveiled its prototype Model 200 a year later, the first two units off the assembly line were delivered to Mullins.

That year, 1948, also saw the arrival of another audio breakthrough: the Neumann U47 condenser microphone, initially marketed by the Telefunken corporation (and hence nicknamed 'The Telly'). The U47 was followed a year later by the M49, the first mic with a remotely-switchable pickup pattern. Highly versatile, and capable of delivering astonishing warmth and clarity, both Neumann models would become the industry's standard mics for both vocal and instrument recording, a position they would hold for decades.

Though wax discs continued to be used as a recording medium into the early 1950s, magnetic tape quickly became the medium of choice. Reel-to-reel tape machines could be stopped and restarted quickly and easily; engineers could edit together several takes of the same song by cutting out the best sections of the tape using a razor blade, then sticking them back together to form a final master. For performing artists accustomed to waiting for a disc change every few minutes, the continuity that tape provided helped maintain the momentum during a recording session.

The real difference, however, was in the dramatically improved fidelity the new equipment offered. The characteristic warmth of the full-bodied Neumann vocal mic lit a fire under the careers of Tony Bennett, Ella Fitzgerald and especially Frank Sinatra (and also permanently closed the ailing big-band jazz era). Within a few short years, sound engineering came of age, as studio engineers developed the art of microphone placement in order to capture the best 'dynamics' of a studio performance. The results of their efforts were – and still are – breathtaking. Responding to consumer demand, equipment manufacturers began designing bigger and better speakers, amplifiers and turntables, launching an unprecedented American hi-fi boom. Having suffered through many a lean year, the record industry sought to cash in quickly. In 1955 alone, vocalist Frank Sinatra – then at the peak of his popularity – had six different albums simultaneously on sale in the record stores.

But, like all previous studio permutations, the new technology had little bearing on the activity on the studio floor. Throughout the early part of the 1950s – the so-called 'golden age' of recording – performers went about their business as they had for years, arriving well rehearsed and cutting upwards of ten sides in a session. Not that they had any choice; though light-years ahead of its predecessor the wax-disc, the prototype tape recorder was still a monaural medium. But in a garage studio in nearby Teaneck, New Jersey, jazz guitarist-turned-inventor Les Paul was perfecting a method for recording musical parts one at a time, rather than together, using an Ampex recorder fitted with an additional playback head. Paul's invention – which he dubbed 'sound on sound' – would ultimately lead to true multi-track recording and change the course of popular music forever.

30 years on
30th street

t's the oldest name in the history of recorded sound – but it took more than longevity to make Columbia Records one of the most powerful labels on the planet. Clean custom consoles, a collection of excellent German microphones, and a large and knowledgeable staff of producers and engineers became the label's hallmarks during the boom years of modern recording.

The label also had an impressive stable of artists: by the end of the 1950s, top vocal acts like Tony Bennett and Johnny Mathis, as well as jazz movers such as Miles Davis and Duke Ellington (who'd launched another in a series of comebacks in 1956 with the live smash *Ellington at Newport*), were just a few of the label's featured players. On the lighter side, Ray Conniff's choruses, Percy Faith's instrumentals (including the mother of all MOR hits, 'Theme from *A Summer Place*') and Mitch Miller's singalong selections kept Columbia on the charts for years on end.

Columbia made the most of its artist roster by constructing a series of top-flight recording studios at various locations around the world. In New York, at one time or another, Columbia had four separate facilities: Liederkranz Hall, on East 58th Street; the 30th Street Studio on East 30th; Studio A at 799 7th Avenue; and a series of studios, including Studio B, near Madison Ave. on 49 East 52nd Street.

Columbia's first was also one of its best: Liederkranz Hall, a converted German beer hall located between Park and Lexington Avenues. Some 100 feet long and 60 feet wide, with 30-foot high ceilings, Liederkranz was an acoustical gem of a studio, offering tremendous, concert-hall style ambience with room to spare; so much so that CBS head William Paley ultimately decided to divide the studio in half, using one portion as a television studio and the other for recording.

Liederkranz wasn't without its drawbacks. During winter months, the studio's old steam radiators made audible pops and whistles, which meant turning the heat off during a long session – not the best solution in the middle of a New York February. Once CBS television moved in, the studio could no longer accommodate the large orchestras that once frequented the hall. In 1949, the record division decided it was time to relocate. Columbia dispatched a team consisting of Bill Bachman, Vin Liebler, and producer George Avakian to scour Manhattan in search of available real estate.

They soon discovered an abandoned Armenian church, 28 blocks downtown at 207 East 30th Street, near 3rd Avenue. The structure was much roomier even than Liederkranz. Though a good distance from the industry's heart in midtown Manhattan, the building was also easily accessible – and, being on the East Side, relatively affordable. A short time later, Columbia's newest recording factory – now named the 30th Street Studio – was open for business.

THE CHURCH

The magical acoustic properties that would soon be 30th Street's trademark would not have been immediately apparent to anyone who first entered 'The Church.' A simple 8 feet by 14 feet control room was located one flight up (later moved to ground level) overlooked a single massive recording room that measured 100 feet around, with 100-foot high ceilings. Drapes left behind by the previous owners hung unceremoniously against the studio's back wall (and were left in place for sound control); rows of long, hanging lights dropped down from the ceiling, so many of them in fact, that a large step-ladder required for the frequent light-bulb changes became a permanent fixture on the studio floor (and is clearly visible on numerous album sleeves).

Mitch Miller, Columbia's head of A&R at the start of the 1950s, immediately saw the enormous potential of 30th Street's palatial interior. Once Miller and the Columbia crew had tweaked the building to perfection, Miller issued a directive strictly prohibiting any kind of physical alteration of the main studio. Janitors weren't even allowed to wash the floors.

Before long, many in the business – in New York and elsewhere – came to regard 30th Street Studio as the best-sounding room of its time. Today, some consider it the greatest recording studio in history.

During its first full decade, 30th Street Studio gave birth to some of the most dynamic-sounding records in the business. Vocal acts flocked there, from Johnny Mathis and Andy Williams to Rosemary Clooney and Barbara Streisand. Tony Bennett cut his first hit, 1950's 'Boulevard of Broken Dreams,' at 30th Street; he recorded almost nowhere else over the next three decades. The sounds of the New York Philharmonic, led by conductor/composer Leonard Bernstein, regularly filled the air; the New Christy Minstrels recorded hootenanny hits; comics and spoken word artists performed there as well. Canadian pianist Glenn Gould recorded his *Goldberg Variations* at 30th Street,

■ CREED TAYLOR **"I did Miles'** *Sketches of Spain* **at 30th Street,** *Big Band Bossa Nova* **with Gary McFarland and Stan Getz was recorded there as well. Those records, like so many others that were made there, had a real identifiable stamp. I can always hear when a record came from 30th Street. It was one of those places with a totally unique sound."**

EARLY RECORDINGS AT 30th STREET STUDIO

GLENN GOULD
Bach *Goldberg Variations*
Recorded June 10-16th, 1955

TONY BENNETT
'Ca C'est L'Amour'
Recorded September 19th, 1957

MILES DAVIS SEXTET
'So What'
Recorded March 2nd, 1959

THE DAVE BRUBECK QUARTET
'Take Five'
Recorded July 1st, 1959

PERCY FAITH ORCHESTRA
'Theme from A Summer Place'
Recorded September 11th, 1959

just hours after inking his Columbia contract in 1955. He returned to 30th Street for a reprise performance just months before his death – and the studio's demise – in 1982.

To get the most out of its new investment, Columbia outfitted 30th Street with the latest in sound-recording artillery, including a vast collection of Neumann U47 and M49 microphones, several Ampex mono and two-track (and later three-and four-track) tape machines, custom consoles outfitted with Pultec EQs and Universal Audio limiters, and Altec 604E playback monitors. The results were uniformly spectacular; on today's equipment, even the most minute details of a 30th Street session – a squeaking piano pedal or a bowed bass string – are clearly audible. But what made 30th Street Studio the envy of the record-making world had less to do with machinery than the composition of the room itself, left virtually untouched from its previous ownership. Unvarnished wood floorboards gave horns and strings their characteristic warmth; to hear 30th Street is to hear drummer Joe Morello's snare and kick-drum shots echoing off the 100-foot ceiling during the percussion break in Dave Brubeck's great 'Take Five,' the first jazz single in history to crack the Top 30 (and with a drum solo, no less).

In 1959, two of the most commercially successful mainstream jazz albums in history – Brubeck's masterpiece of compound time, *Time Out*, and Miles Davis' majestically melodic *Kind of Blue* – were recorded just weeks apart at 30th Street Studio. Coincidence? Perhaps – but probably not. By 1959, Columbia had compiled a team of skilled producers and engineers who'd learned how to capture effectively the sounds of 30th Street's vast interior, among them Teo Macero, Fred Plaut, Harold 'Chappy' Chapman, Ernie Altschuler and Robert Waller. No one, however, understood the complexities of 30th Street Studio better than its resident sound craftsman and the only engineer whose career began with wax and ended with 24 tracks: Frank Laico.

THE EPIC CAREER OF FRANK LAICO

As one of seven children raised in upper Manhattan during the Depression, making records for a living was hardly at the top of Laico's agenda. "We all suffered during that time, and my suffering was having to leave high school to help support the family," says Laico. While he was working as an apprentice at a butcher shop in the Bronx, Laico was approached by a customer who was the treasurer for the World Broadcasting Corporation. "He said, 'Are you thinking of doing this for the rest of your life?' I told him I really wasn't, and so he asked me to come up to the house. He said there was an opening at World Broadcasting, but that he wanted to make sure I really wanted to change my line of work before he offered me the job. I told him I'd do it. So I went to work at World Broadcasting, at 711 5th Avenue, running their mimeograph machine."

The seeds of Laico's impending career were sown one day in 1939, when he found himself up on the building's 13th floor. He heard music playing from behind a pair of closed doors. "It was the recording room," says Laico. "There were these 16-inch wax platters going around, this group performing. It all sounded great! I was fascinated by the whole place. I kept going back in there, and eventually they showed me how to drop the cutter – a real sensitive operation, working with wax, you know – until finally I approached them about the possibility of working in there full time. They agreed – I started as an apprentice, which meant I got to take home an additional two dollars a week. But I got my feet planted."

When the war intervened, Laico wound up at US Recording in Washington, DC, working on military electronics and continuing to hone his skills. Before he could get shipped over to Europe, however, Laico sustained a foot injury while playing baseball. It prevented him from seeing active duty. "It was an act of God," says Laico.

During that time Columbia had been renting space from World because it didn't yet own its own cutting facilities. "I was the guy in the cutting room doing their

■ **ROY HALEE (CBS producer, Simon & Garfunkel, Lovin' Spoonful) "Frank Laico was one of the all-time, really fine mixers. No question about it. A great engineer. He had the 30th Street Studio in his back pocket. I was always very uncomfortable going into 30th St. myself. You had to control the leakage in that place, because it was a big church, you had to have the savvy. Consequently you could talk at one end of it and hear whispers on the other side. I would tend to get excited and panic with all that ambience, given the kinds of sessions I was doing. Too live for me. So I wouldn't go in there unless I was trying to do something special. But Frank had that place locked up. He could take anyone in there and get a really fine sound. He really knew how to control those acoustics."**

■ **DAVID RUBINSON (CBS producer for Moby Grape, Chambers Brothers) "Frank Laico was a real prince – one of the nicest people I ever met. I learned so much from Frank. He did everything – Mathis, Miles, Miller, Bennett, everything. When I first arrived at Columbia, I was 20 years old, and I was a lunatic. He was the last of Columbia's great team of engineers that had started out years before."**

masters," says Laico, "and their boss at the time, Vin Liebler, suggested that he might have work for me when I got out of the service. I told him thanks, I'd consider it."

When World wouldn't agree to a salary increase, Laico resigned, embarking on a series of temporary jobs that eventually led him to the door of Liebler. "I walked in and he said, 'I knew you'd be back.' He hired me on the spot. As it turns out, it was the perfect time to be in the business."

Right from the start, Laico made it clear that he wasn't content to remain a cutter exclusively. "I told them that my real ambition was to get into the studio and do some creative work, using my knowledge and my ears, and so I made that a condition of my employment. Liebler didn't promise me anything, but he didn't say no either. When they got a new supervisor from Chicago, I immediately approached him with the prospect of working inside the studio. He agreed to let me start finding my way around."

The site of Laico's passage into the studio world was 799 7th Avenue, Columbia's main recording facility in 1946. There he began "filling in" – wiring and hanging microphones, moving equipment around, and so forth. "Just so I could get the feel of the studio," says Laico, "setting up the mics based on where I thought they should go, to learn to mix it all in one fell swoop. But I'd been given that opportunity. It was all intuitive – at that point, tape hadn't even arrived, we were still cutting to disc. Although we did do some overdubbing by taking two discs of the same material using three turntables that stayed in sync – which they never did very well anyway. So the idea was to get it right all at once, of course.

> "AT THE SAME TIME AS HE WORKED ON HIS GROUNDBREAKING MULTI- TRACK TAPE RECORDER, LES PAUL DISCOVERED TAPE ECHO."

"When tape came along, we then had to learn how to splice, how to keep them in sync as well – because in those days they didn't have motors that you could just lock in. We had to have two tape recorders at all times – one for the safety back-up, which would always be immediately sent to the vault and maintained at a direct and constant temperature in the event of some mess-up with the master tape. By 1949 or 1950 we had a lot of the standard equipment available. But it wasn't just about the equipment, you also had to have the personnel. At one point we had as many as 110 guys working in the department – cutters, editors, maintenance, other studio people."

With three years of service to his credit, Laico was well positioned when the Armenian church on East 30th Street was transformed into Columbia's newest recording facility in the fall of 1949.

"When we first started at 30th Street, believe it or not, we didn't even have a control room," recalls Laico. "We had these class 'A' phone lines going all the way up to the recorders at Columbia's 52nd Street studio. But then it became such a popular spot, not only for groups but for the vocalists, that we turned it into a full-service studio."

THE INNOVATIVE LES PAUL

The same year 30th Street commenced operations, in nearby Teaneck, New Jersey, guitarist-inventor Les Paul figured out a way to add multiple parts to a recorded backing track by outfitting an Ampex tape recorder with an additional playback head. Paul called his invention "sound on sound," and in 1951 demonstrated the device with a multi-guitar rendition of the jazz standard 'How High the Moon,' featuring his wife, Mary Ford, on vocals.

Paul's idea would ultimately change the course of popular music; by the mid 1960s, tape machines capable of recording sound onto eight separate tracks had become standard issue in recording studios around the globe. To the classical, jazz and vocal performers of the early 1950s, however, such sound embellishment was superfluous. Though various studios purchased the earliest Paul-designed, Ampex-built three- and four-track machines, few actually used them.

Paul's explorations didn't end there. While working on the multi-track, he simultaneously discovered "tape echo," whereby a signal from one tape head was fed to a second machine running at a slower speed, then returned to the original. Tape echo nicely replicated the actual reflections found in reverberant rooms, but Paul took the invention one step further. During the 1940s, Chicago-based engineer Bill Putnam had popularized the use of live echo chambers, isolated rooms made of reflective plaster or tile that enhanced the sound of a dry signal fed to the room through a basic loudspeaker. Paul – who constructed his own echo chamber on a hillside adjacent to his New Jersey home – experimented by delaying the signal to the chamber, which created an ethereal 'splashing' effect.

"Early on at 30th Street, singers, especially, would want something on their voice," says Laico. "We realized that we couldn't always do it by just using the room. So we went down into the basement and looked around. We opened these doors, and there it was – this nice room that had been used by the church for storage. It had a bunch of junk in it, but it was solid concrete. And I said to Mitch [Miller], 'Why can't we use this?' So Mitch had Ed Sorensen and his boys come down, put in speakers and mics and wired it up into the control room. We didn't have to do anything to it, really – we just kept it nice and dry in there.

"We kept experimenting with the mics and the speakers – we tried different types of speakers, moved them into different positions and so forth. We started with an RCA 44 ribbon mic, then we went to a Neumann U47 soon after that. That was the one we ended up sticking with for good, actually. At one point we wound up putting carpeting under the mic stand to cut down on any problems that might occur at louder levels. Once we got it to where it sounded really good, we just left it – with the strict rule that it couldn't be touched!"

Though it sounded downright monumental on record, the storage room that Laico and Miller transformed into one of the finest natural live chambers in the world was anything but. "It was about 12 feet wide by about 15 feet long, with a low ceiling, maybe seven or eight feet high at best," says Laico. Even when all the instruments were being fed to the chamber, Laico could regulate the degree of echo by raising or lowering the fader volume of the individual sections. "Every mic would have its own 'send' position, and you'd just set it at the level that suited you – you could isolate that mic to see how it sounded without the rest of the group, then blend it back in. And you could regulate the return as well. It worked amazingly well.

"Mitch was good friends with Les Paul," says Laico, "and one time he came back from a visit to Les's place in New Jersey, and he said, 'You know, Les has got this thing he does with his echo where he puts a tape delay in front of it, maybe we should try it. What do you think?' I thought it sounded like a great idea, so once again we called in maintenance crew, they set it up, we repositioned everything again – and there it was. It had the effect of really smoothing out the sound of the chamber. If you listen to a chamber on its own and you hear the return, it just sort of dies. The delay not only gave it warmth, it also increased the length of the decay as well. It was such an important discovery."

In many instances, the effect was tailored to fit the style of the individual performer. "We could vary the amount of the delay to the chamber, we tried different variations of EQ as well," says Laico. "For instance, once we'd honed Mathis' vocal sound – ie, the amount of echo, shades of EQ, where the mic was situated in the chamber, etc – we'd mark it down, and, presto, that would be the formula for him. Same for Tony Bennett. It's the reason why his records have such a familiar sound."

Between the palatial main room and the adjustable echo-sends of the downstairs chamber, 30th Street offered a myriad of sound possibilities. "Even if you didn't want a massive reverb through the live chamber, you could have that warm spacious quality that the room provided. After a while, producers from around the world began visiting, wanting to know what we were doing in order to get that sound," notes Laico, "when in reality it was just this concrete bunker, with a speaker, a U47, and a bare light bulb!"

Though he'd frequently work sessions at Columbia's other locations, Laico couldn't come close to capturing the sound that his 30th Street chamber provided. "At 799 7th Avenue, we began experimenting with the rear stairwell that ran down to the basement floor, for the purpose of creating echo," says Laico. "That actually worked quite nicely. The problem was that you'd also pick up the sounds of people walking around in the building, the elevator going up and down, and so forth. So basically the only time you could really use it effectively was late at night when nobody else was around. But that was a good one, all right. In fact, it was Roy Halee who really made the most of that set-up. He deserves a lot of credit for that."

Near the end of the 1950s, Germany's EMT corporation introduced its 'echo plate,' an electronically generated echo device that simulated the sound of live echo by sending a recorded signal through a transducer across a long metal plate housed within a large box. With the arrival of the EMT 140 reverb unit, many engineers abandoned live chambers all together – but not Laico.

"When the plates started coming in during the early 1960s, Columbia's head of research came down and said, 'You know, you should really use these things. They're great, they sound better than the chambers.' He really sold the company on it. But I never really used them at 30th Street. They put them in at 799 7th Avenue and later on up at 49 East 52nd Street, but for me, it was always that chamber. There was just no suitable substitute. At 49 East 52nd Street we outfitted a room to use as a live chamber

■ **MALCOLM ADDEY (engineer for EMI in London) "It took EMI engineers years of studious nipping-and-tucking to finally arrive at the desired echo balance and tonality that you hear on those Beatles records. To tell you the truth, we were really after Columbia's sound – at one point we even went over to the 30th Street Studio to find out what they did to make those records sound so special. And actually, we got pretty close to it."**

■ **STAN ROSS (engineer and founder of Gold Star Studios) "All the Columbia records made in New York during that time had the most wonderful echo sound, and it was because they had these beautiful echo chambers there. I used to love to hear that on a recording – so, right away, that was something we wanted to have on our own productions."**

but it never really responded the way we wanted it to," says Laico. "I'd use it sometimes, but it never really came close to the 30th Street chamber. Which of course had to do with the acoustics of the studio at 30th Street itself. Because the quality of the sound you send into the chamber determines the kind of sound you're going to get back."

As one who spent each week working in the vast confines of 30th Street, it's no surprise that Laico fought against the close-miked, room-deadening trend that came to dominate the industry in later years. When recording piano, Laico situated his 49s several feet above the top of the instrument. Rather than use iso-booths, Laico – who detested sound separation – simply placed vocalists in the center of the floor directly in front of the backing band. "And when it came time for vocal overdubs, unless they insisted on headphones, I'd just put a big monitor speaker right next to them, and adjust the level. You always get a truer performance that way. Even that touch of leakage from the backing track can be nice."

> "COLUMBIA BECAME THE LABEL THAT GOT THE BUSINESS GOING FULL SWING. WE WERE PIONEERS, BASICALLY. IT WAS A GREAT TIME TO BE IN THE BUSINESS."

Laico also concocted an entirely unique use for the studio's portable baffles. "I used to take some of the horn players," says Laico, "and put them just a bit apart from the rest of the group. I'd face the hard side of the baffling towards them, then put a mic between the players and the bafflings – and pick off the sound as it bounced off that baffling surface! You'd get this nice little echo effect right there in the studio."

In many ways, it's what Laico didn't do that resulted in such a powerful body of work. "Once everything was set up, and we got the best take," says Laico, "that was it. To all intents and purposes, the record as you now know it was complete."

Case in point: Tony Bennett's 'If I Love Again,' recorded on the evening of October 19, 1962. Inside 30th Street's recording room, Bennett stood before a suspended M49 microphone, with pianist Ralph Sharon to his right, drums and upright bass to his left, and a contingent of string players situated directly behind him.

After adjusting the microphones, Laico went back into the control room, where, during a run-through of the song, he set up a stereo mix that essentially mirrored the arrangement of the musicians as they appeared through his control-room glass. With the exception of some live reverb from the studio's basement echo chamber, little else was added during the take itself.

Cue up the 42-year-old track this evening, and what you'll hear through your speakers is exactly what Laico heard through his Altec speakers on that late-fall evening on Manhattan's Lower East Side.

Four decades later, Columbia recordings like 'If I Love Again' haven't just stood the test of time; in many instances, their distinctively atmospheric quality puts them leagues ahead of the supposedly technically superior recordings of the current era.

"Thanks to the vision of people like Mitch and Goddard Lieberson, Columbia really became the label that got the record business going full swing," says Laico. "There's no doubt about that whatsoever. We were pioneers, basically. It was a great period of time to be in the business."

INTERVIEW **MITCH MILLER and FRANK LAICO**

He spent more than half his life inside a control room, so it's not surprising that Frank Laico still likes to be in control. "Get over into the right lane, you're going to miss the exit!" he barks as we career through New York's Upper West Side on our way to meet his former boss, recording-industry legend Mitch Miller. "I used to take this route every day – after I stopped taking the train in," recalls Laico. As it turns out, Laico owed his new transport arrangements to Miller, who in 1962 gave his ace engineer a Volkswagen Beetle as a reward for more than 15 years of service. "It was just what I needed," he recalls. "Perfect for parking."

I first met Frank in 1999 while researching an article about the history of echo chambers. I'd known about his work since I was a kid; as a basement engineer (with a fondness for echo), I considered him a giant. I began making regular trips to Frank's home in Westchester County, New York, to discuss his numerous studio exploits.

It was Frank who said, "If you're doing a book about New York, of course you'll have to speak to Mitch." Though best known for his *Sing Along With Mitch* albums and TV shows, featuring old-time favorites performed by his male chorus and orchestra, Mitch Miller is in fact one of the most important figures in the history of popular music. A trained oboe player, he toured with Gershwin straight out of college in the 1930s, then worked sessions with Charlie Parker a decade later. As Columbia's top A&R man, hired by an old friend, then-CBS president Goddard Lieberson, in 1950, Miller turned his label's pop division into an empire, signing and cultivating one hit artist after another.

He also made a few celebrated goofs, most notably forcing Frank Sinatra to record. novelty tunes, and later turned a blind eye to the rising rock'n'roll movement. But with Laico, Miller crafted Columbia's instantly recognizable vocal sound, its greatest legacy. "They should build a statue to Mitch Miller at 57th and Broadway," remarked Jerry Wexler, an early admirer. "Before Mitch came along, pop music was vestigial, strings-behind-potted-palms; he changed all that. He threw out the 32-bar form; he used bastard instruments. He was the first great record producer in history. What they did at that church under his regime was some of the most incredible music ever made."

Since Laico had set up the meeting with Miller, now 93 and and living in the same spacious Park Avenue apartment he had bought back in 1960, I suggested he join us for the interview.

Could you describe a typical day at the office, 30th Street Studio, circa 1960?

MITCH MILLER We would go in, and in one day make a 12-sided album. And you listen to them today and they sound fabulous! And it's because everybody there knew exactly what they were doing, instead of correcting whatever stupid mistakes they made during the recording, which has been the case for many years. The problem is that they're using the technology as a crutch, rather than a tool. Or, when half the guys on the record haven't even met each other. They're record carpenters, not record producers. And you can't get any excitement out of a recording when you're working like that. Then there's the matter of unlimited tracks. Realistically, why should it take four guys 48 tracks to make a decent recording?

Today, the term 'producer' suggests someone with technical ability, but that wasn't always the case.

I, for one, knew nothing about technique, I'd just tell Frank what I wanted to hear and he'd invariably get it for me. Not that I didn't understand how it all worked. Back then I used to hate compression, because the volume on your record would be dictated by the highest point on the record. If you had just one peak, the rest of the record would be down low. So what we used to do is manually rig it, so that when we got to the peak, we'd drop the level, which prevented the compression from kicking in and kept the volume up. Back then, you had to be sure to really pump up the bottom – because the first thing you'd lose was the bottom, the bass and the rhythm section. That's why the Columbia records would be the loudest records on the jukebox! Simple, obvious things like that – but they worked. The ears are the easiest thing to deceive.

30th Street was such an immense room. Surely it must have scared a lot of engineers away?

FRANK LAICO Early on, no one knew that 30th Street had this magical acoustic quality.

MILLER It was made of wood flooring and plaster, and about 100 feet high. Incredible. That's really why the best places were the churches, when you come right down to it. And it wasn't just the shape of the room, it was also what the room was made of. Like the age of the wood, for instance. Which is why we never even did any kind of maintenance in there – no cleaning, no painting, nothing!

LAICO That was one of Mitch's stipulations right from the start. Even those drapes that you see in the photographs – they were hanging there like that when we arrived. But all the time Mitch was there, they stayed right in that spot.

MILLER Symphony Hall in Boston used to be this amazing-sounding space, then about 25 years ago they decided to clean the floors with a mop. Just from the water going into the wood, the sound changed completely. Well, it's like with any great wooden instrument: you know that you don't mess with the finish. So if that's the case with a violin, wouldn't the same principle apply to a large wooden room?

You had such a range of artists, and yet the overall sound was consistent throughout – big acoustics, echo with the delay, that kind of thing.

LAICO There were some differences. Depending on who the artist was, we might not use the same amount of echo as the previous artist, for instance. A lot of it was determined by what was happening in the room during the session, and how it all related to the overall sound. And it worked, because the performance was happening right there in front of you, completely live. When you could hear it all at once like that, you knew immediately how much effect you'd need, how to place the instruments in the stereo field, and so forth.

MILLER The point is, what we were hearing at that moment in the control room is what you hear when you put on the record today. That phenomenon doesn't exist any more, and hasn't for years. It doesn't matter what's going on during the recording, because they've brought in all this stuff – it could be a gorilla in there, it wouldn't matter.

What were you using for playbacks?

As Frank will tell you, we were really the first to listen to the playbacks on these little radio speakers, because that's how people driving around in their cars were hearing the music. That was so important; it enabled us to hear how it would sound in that situation. I mean, if it sounded good through those speakers, then we knew we really had it. Oddly enough, if you made it so that it worked through a car radio, it invariably sounded good through anything – big speakers, small speakers, big room, anywhere. Plus, if it sounded great at low levels, it could only sound better once you cranked the volume.

I still think those Tony Bennett records sound the best on AM – the radio compression, the way it's mixed, it just has that right dynamic element.

I mean, if you've got these huge incredible-sounding speakers in the studio, everyone's sitting there going, "Oh, wow, fantastic, man!" They're all in there jerking off to this great sound [laughs]. And then you hear it on the radio in the car, or at home on one of those little table-top jobs, and suddenly there's no level! No rhythm section! Where are you then?

Were you aware of the impact of your studio techniques on the rest of the recording world?

LAICO I do remember at one point some engineers coming in from Europe so they could see what we were doing in the studio to try and get that sound.

Which happened to be the folks from EMI, who returned to Abbey Road studios and tweaked their chambers just in time for the arrival of the Beatles.

MILLER And that was a great-sounding studio they had over there.

And the same for the guys who worked at Gold Star studios in California, where Phil Spector made his "wall of sound."

Which was to some degree an imitation of what we were doing.

So it would appear that all roads do lead back to Columbia during this time?

We didn't have time to listen to any other records, to hear how we were influencing others. I know RCA was trying to figure it out at one point.

By the time of Percy Faith's 'Theme from A Summer Place' you had stereo – and you had that room completely mastered.

LAICO Harold Chapman – 'Chappy' – did that session. The oboe and the English horn in that studio sounded just … . Well, you can sure hear it on that one!

MILLER Once Chappy got a sound, he wouldn't change it for anything!

That record has so many unusual elements: the picked violin strings with the delayed echo, and those French horns.

LAICO That was Mitch – he was the first one to use French horn on a session like that.

You ended up having an enormous amount of success with Johnny Mathis, even though it took a little while to figure out the right formula for him.

Mitch called me up and said, "We're going to record Johnny Mathis, but we're not going to bother putting anything down until we get a sound." At that point, Johnny had done two albums with George Avakian, trying to be jazz but failing miserably. And borrowing from just about everybody. It had no focus.

MILLER Lena Horne once said, "He stole everything but my gowns." [laughs] And then the albums didn't sell, and Johnny's manager, Helen Noga, comes in, and she's literally crying, she doesn't know what to do. So almost in self-defense, I said to Helen, "Look, give me enough time, we'll go in and do four songs and see what we can do about it." So we came up with 'Chances Are,' 'It's Not For Me to Say,' 'Wonderful! Wonderful!' and 'The Twelfth of Never.' And we honed those songs. 'Wonderful! Wonderful!' was rewritten three or four times.

Really? Was that common?

Absolutely! So many times the writers would have the song, and it might work up to a point, but then maybe the bridge didn't quite make it. You'd lose people if you left it that way. But these writers were real craftsmen, I'd tell them what I'd need, they'd go off and a half-hour later come back with it, completely revamped. No argument.

LAICO So when we started the session, we spent about two hours at least, just developing a sound on his voice. Once we got it, Mitch said, "That's it, leave it."

MILLER Many times, I'd be out in the vocal booth, working with the singers. I mean, Frank could've run the sessions, he didn't need me in there at that point. The thing is, all these singers had this trademark vocal sound, and half the time, you had to remind them what it was. With Mathis, it was this 'choir boy' quality. And once we honed in on that, it just clicked.

So, what you're saying is that it wasn't always the technical aspects of the recording – mic placement, type of mic, etc – that made the session work?

Exactly! Once you set the standard, then the mic will capture it. No microphone ever made a hit.

LAICO But what did matter was the atmosphere of the room. And in the case of 30th Street, that room made those records. Which might sound strange, but it's true. Mitch's sing-along records never would have been hits had they been recorded some place else.

Those Sing Along With Mitch records really set the tone for the "chorale" sound that you hear throughout the 1950s and early 1960s, particularly on those Ray Conniff and Ray Charles Singers recordings.

MILLER Conniff was a reformed alcoholic and out of work, and he asked for a chance. So I gave him those first few Mathis recordings. And right away, he became successful.
LAICO Later on, after he'd moved out to California, he still came back to New York to cut records at 30th Street. Because that was his sound – he couldn't get it anywhere else.

In many instances there is a noticeable difference between the sound of L.A. and New York – and at some point you have to wonder whether it's the construction of the rooms or the actual difference between the two cities in general.
At one point, Vin Liebler came to me and asked if I'd be interested in becoming manager of Columbia's Hollywood studio, which they'd just opened. I was about to go visit my brother, who lived out there at the time, so I told him I didn't know if I'd like L.A., but since I was going out there anyway I'd check it out. When I got there I stood on the curb near where the studio was – and I never saw a soul! It was like being out in the desert. I told my wife I couldn't live there, and that was that.

One of the most notable members of Columbia's roster in the early 1950s was Frank Sinatra, who recorded at 30th Street but never really found his groove.
MILLER History will verify this, but at the time, Sinatra was down on his luck – the church was after him, he'd lost his TV show, he was chasing after Ava Gardner, and he was also having trouble with his voice. Sinatra had a very fragile voice – if he didn't take care of it, it just cracked. I knew all of this, and I did really try to help him – at one point, I let him come in and sing over a previously recorded backing track, which was really against the rules at the time. We were doing this at the 7th Avenue studio, and on disc. Not even tape!

You'd done overdubs with Patti Page ...
Yes. 'Confess' was the first record with vocal multiple tracks. Ask Les Paul!

What was the final break with Sinatra?
The thing with Sinatra was that you always had to jump through hoops for him. At one point he'd refused to record two songs, 'The Roving Kind' and 'My Heart Cries for You.' He'd flown in from the West Coast on his way to Spain to see Ava, who was schtupping the bullfighter [a celebrated matador who performed under the name of Dominguin] and he was furious. He came in at night with his Mafioso group, and he was going to do the session and fly off to Europe. I played him the songs and he said, "I'm not going to do that shit," and walks out. So there I am, the musicians had been hired, so I ended up grabbing

this kid who was sleeping in the publishers office, who turned out to be Guy Mitchell, who cut both of those songs. And they both ended up going to the top of the charts. But that was it for Sinatra. We loaned him a quarter of a million dollars to pay his taxes, and then he did *From Here to Eternity*, paid his public penance, and suddenly his records began to sell. Meanwhile, all the records he said I'd ruined his career with, he started making royalties on.

How connected was the New York Mafia to the record business at that time?
Percentages were being paid to certain people – and for quite a long time, too. It was just part of the atmosphere. I can tell you that during the Korean War when everything was short, we always had plenty of Parmesan cheese and olive oil! [laughs]
LAICO And cigars. My wife always knew when I'd been doing a Mitch session – she could smell it!

In addition to all these major vocal artists, you had a sizable jazz contingent as well: Miles Davis, Gil Evans, Dave Brubeck, Duke Ellington, Thelonious Monk, Stan Getz, John Coltrane.
The Gil Evans sessions were great; you knew you were hearing something that no one else had ever done before. Musicians loved being in on those sessions; you had to really be on your toes. I loved the Ellington sides. Duke would just come in and want to record, and it's not like there was any real producing, you'd just sit there and record him. All the magic was coming out of him.

30th Street also became the most sought-after studio for specialty releases – you did an amazing number of soundtrack albums there, for instance. And Christmas music as well: all those Coniff albums, Mathis, Streisand, Andy Williams.
Once again it was the sound of the studio. I remember during the 1970s Don Costa brought in [arranger] Gordon Jenkins to do a Christmas album for this female Japanese artist. And I asked Don why she had come all the way over here, and he said, "Because they wanted that sound."

A big part of that 'sound' was the method you used to record the vocals in that studio. It didn't necessarily matter what the orchestration was like, either.
MILLER And some of the best material was small group, in fact. Like the Mathis album, *Open Fire, Two Guitars*, which was an idea we worked up right there in the studio [with guitarists Al Caiola and Tommy Mottola, and bassist Milt Hinton], all completely

improvised, no arrangement. The point is, the voice has this wonderful surrounding, but it's not big and overwhelming. A lot of people wanted it like that.

Were all of the Tony Bennett recordings done completely live?
Never did an overdub.
LAICO Same here.

Even well into the late 1970s?
I was there the whole time, and it was always live.

Did you have a favorite mic?
In general, the 49 really became my mic-of-choice. It had such a nice sound – lots of warmth, good mid-range. People always think you have to have a ton of high end, but that's ridiculous. You'd have to be careful with them, they're very delicate, and they'd go out of phase pretty easily as well.

Would you use compression during the recordings?
I would, but not overall, like a lot of people would. You'd really have to some of the time, depending on who you were working with. If you used it properly, it was fine. There's compression on some of those Miles Davis recordings. I would have a compressor on Tony – but only working to the point that it was hardly working at all. So that it doesn't close in everything. I don't like it when everything is compressed – a lot of guys would compress the whole band, then run it all back to the tape like that.

Bennett had an incredibly successful run: 30 straight years, and nearly all of it at 30th Street. By his own admission, he simply wouldn't record anywhere else. What do you think accounts for his longevity?
MILLER My whole theory was to never make an artist a purveyor of just one kind of song. Which is why I was never opposed to throwing in a novelty song here and there. Why not? My model for that idea was Bing Crosby, who did just about everything. What these artists didn't always understand was that I had just as much interest in their success as they did. And Tony wanted to be a jazz artist right away, from the moment we first signed him. And my response was, "Once you get yourself established, you can do anything. But if you miss now, you're dead." But he'd have his mind made up about certain things. Like when we did 'Rags to Riches.' Frank will remember, right at the end when he goes for that last phrase, [sings] "It's up to you," he's a little flat. He said, "If you release that record you'll

ruin my whole career." C'mon! The people made their mind up about the song after the first 20 seconds.

I think that's a good point – it's the case that a lot of Bennett's records sound great right from the top.
A big part of the formula is in the arrangement. We would have it so that what you heard in the introduction kept repeating throughout the record. It takes real skill to do that successfully. Percy Faith was great at that. There's a feeling of wholeness about it.

Whose idea was it to have that finger snap at the beginning 'Ca C'est L'Amour'?
I did that. Afterwards, actually [laughs].

Really? That's you, as an overdub?
Yeah, I would do things like that. Like on Frankie Laine's 'Moonlight Gambler,' I overdubbed the sound of those horse's hoofs – clip clop, clip clop – to give it that feeling of loneliness. [He laughs.]

With Tony Bennett's 'Cold, Cold Heart,' you managed to score a pop smash using a country cover – the first time that ever really happened.
Tony didn't want to have anything to do with that one – he told me, "I'm not doing any cowboy songs." So I says to him, "Idiot [laughs], listen to those last two lines – 'Why can't I free your doubtful mind and melt your cold, cold heart' – and tell me where else you're going to find a better lyric than that!" So he did it.

And it spent six weeks at Number One.
I guess that's one cowboy song that turned out OK!

INTERVIEW **TONY BENNETT**

On April 17th, 1950, Anthony Dominick Benedetto – better known as Tony Bennett – first took his place behind the mike at Columbia's 30th Street Studios in lower Manhattan for a heavily Italianized take on 'The Boulevard of Broken Dreams.' It would be the first in a string of early 1950s pop hits. Bennett matured rapidly, and with help from sidemen Count Basie, Zoot Sims, and other greats, began moving in a more jazz-based direction. Right from the start, Columbia engineer Frank Laico, mastermind of 30th Street, treated Bennett's vocals with a rich, toppy echo that demanded attention and rendered Bennett's recordings among the most stately in all of pop music. Bennett hit a commercial high in late 1962 when he took the Douglas Cross and George Cory composition 'I Left My Heart in San Francisco' into the Top 20, scoring a pair of Grammys and gaining a 'signature' song in the process.

Over the next 20-odd years, Bennett fought a fickle market, conquered a serious chemical addiction, but never completely faded from view. Though the hits stopped coming, Bennett remained a consistent concert draw, who continued to reward his audiences with top-flight material. Through it all, Bennett refused to knuckle under to the pressures of the pop market; instead, he patiently trod the commercial waters, continued to record with jazz dignitaries, and even tried his hand at launching an independent label.

Not everyone could see it coming, but Bennett had one late, great comeback in him. It began auspiciously enough with 1986's *The Art of Excellence*, Bennett's first record in five years, then continued with 1990's acclaimed *Astoria: Portrait of the Artist*. Before long, Bennett was back in the spotlight, still in great voice, ready to take on a whole new audience.

Capitalizing on the 'lounge' trend of the early 1990s, Bennett's son Danny, his manager since 1979, presented his dad to the Gen-X market through a succession of high-profile gigs like the *MTV Music Awards* and *The Simpsons*. The veteran crooner handled the newfound adulation with aplomb, dueting with pals Elvis Costello and k.d. lang one moment, chumming up to the Red Hot Chili Peppers the next. It worked brilliantly. Twentysomethings struck by the sight of this oldster bellowing "Givit away! Givit away now!" in Flea's ear tuned in to Bennett's 1994 comeback-capping *MTV Unplugged*; the companion album flew to the top of *Billboard*'s jazz charts, scored an album-of-the-year Grammy and, in 2000, went platinum, reaching the million mark two days shy of the singer's 74th birthday.

In late 2001, Bennett marked his 50th year as a recording artist (35 of them with Columbia) with the Phil Ramone-produced *Playing With My Friends: Bennett Sings the Blues*, featuring duets with Sheryl Crow, Billy Joel, Stevie Wonder, Ray Charles, Bonnie Raitt, and others. His secret? "I didn't change a thing," says Bennett. "And the people finally caught up."

Over the course of your career, you could take nearly everything you recorded in the studio right to the stage and have it come out pretty much the same, minus whatever vocal effect you were using during the recording.

Or even the other way around. In fact, a lot of times we'd break in a song on the road. Like

'San Francisco,' for instance. We'd been performing that song live for a real long time, so when we finally got it into 30th Street Studios, we knocked it off in two takes! Back in the old days, Frank Laico and I were always on a budget, which meant that we had to cover four sides in three and a half hours. We had to be good and tight, and working the material out on the road was a big part of that.

You've always made a point of crediting Frank for helping to define your sound. Engineers don't usually get that kind of recognition.

It just would not have been the same without him. He worked that studio like an artist. And not just for me. Streisand, Mathis, Williams – Frank made all of their hits. Ellington, Leonard Bernstein … I was just lucky to have him with me at the studio all those years.

You used the stage to learn the songs.

Right. Sometimes we'd take a song and play it live for a very long time without even thinking about recording it. Then someone might come up and say, "Hey, I really like that number you guys have been doing, you should record it." We'd suddenly realize we'd been working on this thing for four years, and we really had it down, it was completely broken in! We'd perfected the tempo, gotten the right feel. When that happens, making a record out of it is so easy.

Louis Jordan used to audition new songs on the road, then record the ones that got the best audience response.

Absolutely! But that's how you do it. That's why Louis's records sold so well. They were good songs, performed really well. That was what you did in the studio back then, anyway. You performed! And he knew right away they were going to be hits, just by the reaction they were getting on the road.

But if you think about it, that's a daring thing to do, to just go out there and play these songs that no one's ever heard before, night after night. By and large, it's just the opposite now. You put out a single, then an album, let radio spin it, then hit the road once the material's familiar enough.

Young people just don't have the kind of training we had: a real vaudeville training, where you were a completely well-rounded performing artist by the time you got into the studio. Unfortunately, most record companies are just built on the premise that you have to make more money than you made the month before. That's not how I work.

In fact, I've always let it be known that I wanted to have a hit catalogue, rather than just a bunch of hit records. And over the last decade or so the catalogue really began to pay off. Sometimes it just takes patience. It took me six months to get the right feel for 'The Shadow of Your Smile.' I knew I wanted to do it, I loved Johnny Mandel, but it just wasn't there at first. Then I heard Dizzy Gillespie's instrumental version of it – just beautiful. So I got into that mode. By the time we did it, it was really messed! But sometimes it just takes that long before you know you're ready to record.

In the studio you were never one to be closed off in an isolation booth.
I didn't need to. Even though 30th Street was this huge place, Frank created this great environment for me. It was just right every time. That's why I recorded there for three decades: it was like a soundstage. And the band would always be right behind me with little separation. It was, in essence, like a stage show.

You're still working that way – on your last album, Phil Ramone had you set up as if you were playing a club, right?
Yes. We were even using hand-held mics to get that concert feel. Phil just let us be natural. We could walk over to the bass or the piano if we felt like it, we weren't blocked off with baffles or anything. It was as live as you could get in a studio.

Your voice is really the featured instrument, with only a small backing band for support. Quite different from the way pop acts have evolved.
Well, for starters, young artists don't really have the kind of stage training that there used to be. They're manufactured by producers who put a whole bunch of props and sounds behind them and try to make it all work. I mean, some of these guys haven't even been on stage and have a hit record. And when they finally get out there, it doesn't sound the same.

It's been going that way for quite some time.
True. Sometimes I think we take for granted how important our musical heritage is in this country. I guess I'm lucky that right now, at the age of 75, I'm selling more records than I ever have before in my career. It means I'm communicating – and keeping these wonderful songs a part of the American musical experience.

You've gotten a lot of credit for your willingness to take this kind of classic American music to a much younger audience.
Well, they deserve it! I mean, they're not hearing it on the radio. A lot of them have no idea who the Gershwins were, or Fred Astaire, or even Ellington. It's important. If I'm helping to keep that repertoire alive through my performances, that's great.

the atlantic story

n 2004, a minority of corporate interests controlled the majority of the world's leading record companies, the result of years of intensive downsizing, streamlining, and consolidation. Despite the Internet-based revolution, the idea of an independent start-up doing battle with the likes of BMG on today's Hot 100 is improbable, if not impossible. But 50 years ago, small record makers not only went head to head with the big companies, they dominated the charts as never before.

Independents had very little money – but they also had very little overhead. A major label required big sales to turn a profit in the face of substantial operating expenses, whereas one smash for an independent could finance an entire stack of new releases. With advances in recording technology paving the way, fortune beckoned on every street corner in midtown Manhattan.

One budding entrepreneur was Ahmet Ertegun, son of the Turkish ambassador to the US, who at the age of 14 was adding his own lyrics to Duke Ellington compositions using the record-cutting machine his mom had bought him. With partner Herb Abramson, a former National Records A&R man, and $10,000 in investment capital from the family dentist, Ertegun launched his fledgling label, Atlantic, in the fall of 1947. Two years later, Atlantic had its first hit with Stick McGhee's R&B smash 'Drinkin' Wine Spo-Dee-O-Dee.' Others followed, including 'Don't You Know I Love You' and 'Fool, Fool, Fool' for The Clovers (both penned by Ertegun under the pseudonym 'Nugetre').

In 1953, former *Billboard* writer Jerry Wexler, who had devised the term 'rhythm and blues' as a substitute for the lamentable 'race' designation, joined the Atlantic team as a partner. Three years later, Ahmet's brother Nesuhi, an ardent jazz fan, came aboard and helped recruit jazz luminaries like Erroll Garner, John Coltrane and Ornette Coleman. "It was very much in our interest to bring black artists to mainstream America," says Wexler. "Because we were a small struggling company and we wanted to expand our territory. And it had a residual effect – it helped to break down the barriers that existed in the music business."

ENTER TOM DOWD

For small-label owners, staying afloat in a business controlled by giants like Columbia and Decca was no easy task; by the early 1950s, the record bins were littered with indie also-rans. Atlantic, however, was clearly different: unlike typical record execs, who knew how to sell but little about what they were selling, principals Ertegun and Wexler were both business-savvy and musically astute. And in Tom Dowd, a 20-year-old New Yorker, the label had a crack engineer who could capture great ideas on tape every time out.

"Dowd," remarked Wexler, "was the architect – he studied the physical configuration of a room like he was a scientist."

In fact, Dowd *was* a scientist – a student of physics, to be exact – who in the mid 1940s became part of the government's secret Manhattan Project. Unknown to Dowd at the time, the group's research – testing the explosive properties of splitting atomic particles – would lead to the development of the first atomic bomb. When the government ruled that it was wrong for him to resume his studies for security reasons, Dowd, a trained bass player, chose music instead.

"In 1947, recording was a completely different art form, because of the limitations of the equipment," says Dowd. "State of the art was to employ a 16-inch table with a lead screw of fixed pitched moving a magnetically motivated needle across a disc that you were cutting directly onto. It was 88 lines per inch. If it was a three-minute song, you had to make it 112 lines, which meant lower volume, a higher likelihood that the record would skip, and so forth. There were major problems with this system."

"Back then, engineers primarily came from radio, and almost without exception recorded using just one mic," says engineer Al Schmidt, an early Dowd associate. "If they wanted to change the balance of the instruments, they'd just move people around in the room. Nowadays boards have 72 inputs; you can use 72 mics if you really want to."

But in those days, the lack of choices generally meant less futzing and more playing. "On average, we were doing about four songs in three hours – in other words, a whole album in nine hours," says Schmidt. "Done. As a result, what you heard over the speakers at the end of the day was exactly what people were going to hear over the radio or on their record players at home. The whole process was that fast."

In the late 1940s and early 1950s, any engineer worth his pay-check knew instinctively how to mix as the recording was going down. "Tommy excelled at that," says Ertegun. "He was unbelievable. Nowadays you just set up all the microphones. You've got unlimited tracks, you can remix for years. But back then, you had to get it right at the point of entry. That's how Tom became great."

Ertegun's life-long assocation with Dowd began one afternoon in 1947 at the Apex Studio on 57th Street. "The studio had this German professor who did the bulk of the engineering," recalls Ertegun. "He was really difficult to work with, wouldn't let us turn up the bass, or touch anything, but we were told he was a master, so we put up with him. The next time we were in there, out walks this kid who looked like he was about 15, and tells us, 'I'm the engineer. The professor can't make it. My name's Tommy Dowd.' And he was running around moving mics, bringing up the drum level … and it all sounded great. And my partner Herb says, 'Man, I think we've got something, this kid knows what he's doing.' From that day forward, he recorded every single record we ever did."

"Tom's contributions to the development of the company were inestimable," continues Wexler. "He made it possible for Ahmet and myself to never have to put our hands on the faders."

Right from the start, Dowd proved that great sounds didn't necessarily require great equipment. During his first six years on board, Dowd made do with a simple Magnacord tape machine, a minuscule four-input console, and a handful of cheap microphones. "When we first got started we didn't have any really nice equipment like Neumann condensers," Dowd told writer Blair Jackson. "We were using [RCA] 44s, 77s, Western Electric 639As – the 'salt shakers' – and Turners. That was about the best variety you could have. Back then a lot of studios were abandoned radio-station rooms – and those were the kind of mics you found at places like that."

Dowd's incredibly diverse career – Charlie Parker early on, Lynyrd Skynyrd a quarter-century later – began with him seated at the controls for Eileen Barton's 'If I Knew You Were Coming I'd Have Baked a Cake.' The National Records track became an international hit, and Dowd was off. "That was how I got to record Bird, Lester Young, Dizzy. They were my heroes – and now here I was making records with them. It was unbelievable."

"In those days, recording techniques were such that there was a pronounced difference between hearing a live performance in a club and hearing the same song on record," says Ertegun. Nevertheless, when tape arrived, in 1949, a doubting Ertegun told Dowd he wanted to keep the disc cutter active for making back-ups – a request he quickly abandoned after hearing the results of the new medium. Says Dowd, "It was huge. Tape just increased our possibilities."

Even before the arrival of Atlantic's first Ampex 300, Dowd was eager to test the parameters of conventional record making. "Back then I was never a one-mic advocate. There was a different intensity between, say, a string bass or an acoustic guitar versus a drum. As a result, I didn't even need to mic the drums – I'd mic the bass instead, and the drums would come through anyway. And then put a mic on the singer. Then when I got into the control room, I'd selectively increase or decrease the volume. The result

■ **FRANK LAICO** "Tommy Dowd did absolutely fantastic work. He was a great engineer. Back then when I was living in White Plains he was in Mamaroneck, and so many times we'd be on the train together going in and out of the city, and we'd be talking about our sessions, how the studios were and whatnot."

was that you could suddenly hear everything, and in detail. People would say, 'How did he do that?'"

THERE WAS NO STUDIO

Dowd's accomplishments are all the more remarkable considering the room Atlantic used to make its earliest recordings, located on the top floor of a wood-framed brownstone above Patsy's Restaurant at 234 West 56th Street. "There was no studio," says Dowd. "The office was the studio – and I just had to make do. The shipping room was on the fourth floor and we were on the fifth. The floor sagged and creaked, and the sloped ceiling had a skylight in the middle of it. The whole office wasn t more than 19 by 28 feet. The walls were treated with plywood. Jerry's desk was next to Ahmet's.

"When it was time to record, we'd stack the desks and push furniture into the halls," says Dowd. "At that point, I was light years ahead of the hand-me-down radio equipment being used. By default, I suppose, I became an innovator. The early Atlantic sessions, when I was still a freelancer, had me experimenting like a madman. I had no choice. Jerry and Ahmet were sticklers for a clean, crisp sound, and I was determined to get it. So we just made it happen. We recorded at night. Office during the day, studio at night. Ray Charles, Ruth Brown, Bobby Darin, all the others – right there in that room."

With Nesuhi Ertegun on board, Atlantic's jazz roster reached epic proportions; new recruits included Herbie Mann, The Modern Jazz Quartet, and the great John Coltrane, who'd later record his magnificent *My Favorite Things* album under Dowd's watch. "John Coltrane and that room on 56th Street, those quartets and quintets – it just fit like a hand in a glove. Dynamically, acoustically, everything. It was like magic."

As Atlantic's fortunes swelled, Dowd pursued newer and even more inventive ways of staying ahead of the crowd. Most studios employed a second machine for safety copies; Dowd took it one step further.

"I began recording the jazz sessions using both a mono machine and a two-track for back-up," says Dowd. "I mean, it didn't cost us anything more than an extra reel of tape to do it both ways. It also meant we were building up a stereo library before stereo had even been invented. When stereo came in, while everyone else was making fake stereo, we already had the real thing."

PIONEERING EIGHT-TRACK

That was just the beginning. In 1956 the Atlantic team relocated one block north to 156 West 57th Street (former colleague Herb Abramson later took over the 56th Street studio, re-naming the facility A-1). A year later, Atlantic become the first label in New

York – or practically anywhere, for that matter – to have eight-track capability.

"As an independent, Atlantic didn't always have to deal with a lot of the red-tape constraints that typified larger record companies," adds producer-arranger Arif Mardin, who joined the company as a Berklee graduate in the 1960s. "As a result, we got to work with some technically advanced equipment years before anyone else. The Ampex eight-track was a very expensive but totally state-of-the-art machine at the time. Les Paul, who devised it, had the first, we got the second one, and the third went to the government, because they had to have everything. We'd be recording people like Sonny Stitt and Freddie Hubbard on the eight-track, as well as many of the pop bands that followed. So when the stereo revolution came, all he had to do was mix it again. That's why those records sound so good today."

At Atlantic's new eight-track facility, skeptics quickly became converts. "We were doing a Ray Charles session shortly after I'd hooked up the eight-track," says Dowd, "and after this one take, Ray asked to hear it back, 'and with a little more bass.' Because I had the bass on its own track, I let him have it – just the bass! He bolts off the piano into the control room, yelling, 'Hey, what is that? What're you doing to my record?' That's when I introduced him to the new machine. In 30 seconds, Ray Charles was addicted to eight-track."

A similar fate befell the songwriting team of Jerry Leiber and Mike Stoller, who'd recently entered into a production agreement with Ertegun and Wexler. "We were doing a Coasters session," says Dowd, "and Jerry and Mike were so used to hearing it in mono, that when I played the stuff back in eight-track, they just flipped. They took to it like ducks to water."

By 1959 the influx of new equipment – coupled with Atlantic's steamrolling record sales – prompted yet another change of address, this time to 11 West 60th Street near Broadway. The new Dowd-designed space included a tracking room roughly 40 feet long and 50 feet wide, with 15-foot high ceilings, and a control room spacious enough to

■ **PHIL RAMONE (producer/engineer)** "**Eight-track was a revolutionary change in the business and in the musicality of New York. And Atlantic had it first.**"

■ **FRANK LAICO** "**When it came to recording technology, major companies like CBS and RCA, that always had to report to a board of some sort, were always behind. It was just the nature of the business. These independents, on the other hand, had no shortage of tracks.**"

house the new Ampex eight-track. Like most studios of note during the 1950s and 1960s, Atlantic had a tell-tale echo sound, the product of a small but unusual live chamber that Dowd and assistant Phil Ihele pieced together using scrap bathroom tile from local construction projects.

"60th Street was a cutting edge facility at the time," says Mardin. "A really good-sized place as well. We could have 20 strings, three guitars, bass, drums, organ, piano, and a vocal group. And we could get them far enough separated that we could still have a great live session. Even with the new modern equipment, Dowd, visionary that he was, made all the decisions about reverb, EQ, level, right there, as the recording was going down."

PLAYING THE FADERS LIKE A PIANO

Of course, more tracks meant more inputs – and during the relocation to 60th Street, Dowd ditched his old board and began work on a completely revamped console that would include Pultec EQs, channel limiters, and a groundbreaking new concept: sliding faders. "The equipment most places were using in those days consisted of hand-me-down stuff from broadcast facilities, including consoles that had these big fat three-inch knobs," says Dowd. "The problem was that you couldn't get two or three under your hands. It wasn't just inaccurate, it was plain stupid. Eventually I found a manufacturer who was making slide wires – faders that were linear instead of cylindrical and traveled five inches up and down. Because of the narrow width of these things, I could fit them into a board half as wide. Which enabled me to put a whole group of faders in two hands, which is what I'd wanted to do all along. Finally, I could play the faders like you could play a piano."

In 1960, The Drifters' chart-topping 'Save the Last Dance for Me' became the first record to use Dowd's freshly implemented tracking facilities. By then, Atlantic's quest for musical diversification had moved well beyond anyone's wildest expectations, yet turning away work was never an option. It was Dowd who bore the brunt of the non-stop studio activity. Throughout the 1950s, in an effort to keep up with demand, Dowd had frequently made use of neighboring facilities such as Fulton Sound (where in 1959 he cut Bobby Darin's 'Mack the Knife'), Capitol Recording Studio and other midtown establishments. Better equipment and a bigger room didn't put an end to Dowd's round-the-clock roving.

"There were just too many occasions when a group like The Coasters had been in all afternoon, and suddenly I get a call notifying me that Mingus was coming down at midnight," laughs Dowd. "But you had to do it! If you didn't, they'd be gone. If those guys were ready to play, you'd better be ready to record."

When Nesuhi Ertegun proposed a meeting between the Eric Dolphy and Ornette Coleman quartets, one afternoon in 1960, Dowd took the subway down 7th Avenue to a recently constructed independent facility located next to Manny's Music on West 48th Street. The studio was called A&R, its owner-operator an ambitious young engineer by the name of Phil Ramone. And that's where we'll go in the next section.

ECHO CHAMBERS

During the 1950s and 1960s, custom consoles, effects units, and other homemade devices helped give a studio its 'signature' sound. But the real calling card for many studios was the echo chamber, a specially designed isolated room made of concrete, tile, hard plaster or other reflective surface, used to add concert-hall ambience to an otherwise arid recording.

"Even now, the echo chambers make it possible to distinguish one studio from another," notes Lou Gonzalez, owner of Quad Recording Studios in New York and Nashville. "For the simple reason that they were live rooms – not machines – and they all had a unique sound."

Beginning with the introduction of hi-fidelity recording in the late 1940s, echo chambers became the chief source of sound enhancement in recording. Constructing them for optimum sound quality was often a hit-or-miss proposition. The resulting reverb effect could vary wildly – or, as one noted engineer put it, "some came out great, some didn't." Some were totally funky rooms, made of hard concrete walls requiring frequent maintenance, such as using heat lamps to prevent the build-up of echo-inhibiting moisture. Yet veteran engineers still argue that the well-built chambers were unparalleled as a reverb source, even by today's standards.

Over the years, plate and spring reverbs, tape delays, and, ultimately, digital reverbs would provide studio engineers with ready-made, easily adjustable echo at the touch of a button. But for many, there's never been an acceptable substitute for a real 'live' chamber.

"In the early years of recording – jazz records and such – they'd simply use the room for ambience, rather than an echo chamber per se," says veteran producer/engineer David Rubinson. "As recording progressed, and as there was much more control over the different elements, they'd put a singer in a booth so they could isolate that part of the performance. But as a result that sound was incredibly dry, so the answer was to create an actual acoustic chamber to get some of that ambience back."

Deceptively small despite their cavernous effect – being anywhere from 10 to 15 feet long on average, with a low ceiling – live echo chambers aped the kind of naturally occurring room reverberation that is found under stairways, in long halls, and especially in tiled bathrooms and shower stalls. In fact the walls of many chambers were made of ceramic tile in order to duplicate that 'bathroom' effect. For years, studio technicians would remedy a case of the 'dries' by recording singers in an adjacent stairwell or some similar 'live' space. (Elvis Presley's 'Heartbreak Hotel' was created in such a setting.) By having a chamber on the premises, engineers could count on a dedicated, controlled space solely for the purpose of adding echo.

Though these rooms came in a variety of dimensions, all were wired up under a fairly uniform system. The source from the microphone amplifier (for instance, a vocal track) was fed to the chamber through a loudspeaker placed in one corner of the room. A microphone situated at the opposite corner (in order to maximize the reverb time) fed the separate signal to the tape machine, where it was mixed into the recorded performance.

One mark of a good chamber would be its maximum reverb time. Top-notch chambers might 'ring' anywhere from five to ten seconds, though usually only half that time could be caught on tape. Adjusting the reverb time, as well as its shape and color, simply became a matter of increasing or decreasing the signal to the loudspeaker, altering its return, or better still, moving the microphone closer to or farther away from the speaker. Just as the echo sends and returns could be manipulated through tape delay, they could also be equalized – hence the various 'shades' of chamber reverb, from the noticeably bright echo sounds (achieved by rolling off all but the highest frequencies to accentuate 's' and 't' vocal sounds) to rounder, darker colorations.

"For years, the whole point of recording was to capture a live event," says Rubinson. "That's why everything sounded so rich and full – you'd be using the properties of the room as part of the technique. Similarly, you'd have the one echo chamber with multiple feeds going into it. You could adjust the individual gains, you could regulate how much was going into it that way.

"If you had stereo reverb, you'd have a mono feed with a stereo return. And with multiple sends, you could send to different types of chambers if you wanted – to an EMT, to a small live chamber, a large live chamber, and so forth. You were using the live chamber as a reverberant device to mix the sound of the entire event – rather than creating a different effect for every single track."

Multiple sounds being fed simultaneously into an echo chamber tended to blend into one colorful pattern, adds Rubinson. "Nowadays you have separate little reverberations on each individual sound, which can be very sterile. But when you'd send all the instruments to the chamber, it would all mix together, you'd get all that phase cancellation, added frequencies and different tones, and it would give the effect of everything being in the same room. That's what made it so rich. And it worked wonders for overdubs – you couldn't tell what had been added later."

The sounds that emerged from the chambers were often the result of haphazard creativity. To control the amount of echo on his recordings, Bill Putnam, a founding father of reverb, put a clothesline pulley inside his chamber, which allowed him to move the microphone back and forth from his control room seat.

"With the chambers, you were forced to try different things," says engineer Frank Laico. "Move the mic around, adjust the level of the speaker, throw down a rug to soften the sound, basic things. But it was always fun to experiment like that."

Though echo chambers became essential apparatus for any studio, a select few were coveted for their superior sound quality. In fact, some of the most popular echo chambers in history were equipped with class 'A' phone lines, so that studios from miles around could patch in live, booking the room as one would reserve regular studio time.

Unfortunately, the demise of the big studios also signaled the beginning of the end of the live echo chambers, which, by the 1980s, were considered too cumbersome to compete in newer, smaller, and more technologically advanced environments. When Lexicon ushered in the digital reverb era in 1978, live echo was suddenly considered hopelessly out of date.

"When everything was being recorded at once, the echo chamber was a key element," says Rubinson. "But as multitracking became the norm, there came the need to control the sound more. At that point studios started using the EMT echo plates, and then stereo plates, and then two or three different plates. And you could move the plate, tune it, dampen it, and so forth. The more you get away from recording everything all at once – which came with three and four-track recording – the more you need to control all the individual sounds."

Today, a few good live chambers still exist, including several at New York's Hit Factory, as well as those at Capitol and A&M studios in Hollywood. But the passing of the echo chamber era – and the advent of the sophisticated multi-track – irrevocably changed a major aspect of studio recording.

"Since the sounds would be fed into the chambers during the performance – rather than after the fact – that to me was the essence of having echo as a live performer," notes Rubinson. "After that, it really became a post-production technique. At that point, the whole concept of using the studio to capture a live event really went out the window."

a studio
called a&r

I n the late 1950s, Phil Ramone was a musical prodigy, a gifted violinist, formally trained at the Julliard School of Music. By that time, however, Ramone had developed a different passion: recording. "After years of performing classical works I started getting into jazz," recalls Ramone, "and I began playing at these small clubs around town. It was the complete opposite of everything I'd learned up until that point – it was like a form of rebellion.

"Anyway, it was from those club dates that I wound up assisting this guy Charlie Leighton, a great harmonica player who owned this little studio called JAC, located on West 58th between 6th and 7th. JAC was basically built out of an apartment, with a living room separated from the hallway by folding curtains. There was this great group of guys that included Charlie as well as his partner Jack Arnold, who would later become my partner. I'd cut discs late at night, help out with any kind of engineering tasks, and so forth.

"The recordings I'd done at JAC were mainly demos," says Ramone. "Once I'd gotten a chance to see real records being made over at these other studios like Coastal Recording, I knew right away what I wanted to do with my life. So that was a beginning. But JAC was a lovely place to get started."

Ramone also realized that the novelty of working as a studio assistant would only last so long. "I'd started out very young," says Ramone, "and I was lucky enough to have people like Don Frey and Bill Schwartau around, who had the presence of mind to hand me the baton when he knew I was ready. At that point, I knew I really had to grow, and Jack Arnold was as crazy as I was, so we decided to build our own studio."

One day in 1959, Ramone found himself inside the Mogul Film Building at 112 West 48th, located next to Jim & Andy's bar. "Manny's Music was on one half of the building; on the other side was a camera store. On the fourth floor there was a sign that said, 'For Rent: Studio Vacant.' I walked in there and there was this wonderful old man who had

■ **BOB LUDWIG (veteran mastering engineer)** **"Phil Ramone was my mentor … He had the best engineers and the best maintenance people; A&R was the cream of the independent studios in NYC during the 1960s. Nothing could touch them back then."**

■ **ROY HALEE (CBS producer/engineer)** **"Being an engineer requires helping out in every way you can, providing the artist isn't acting like a complete jerk. I've seen Phil in situations at A&R that the average guy would crack under, and he'd sail right through it."**

all these old cameras, vintage silent films, and all this other stuff that museums used to sub-let from him. I somehow managed to talk him into letting us rent the available space from him, with some small guarantees. A friend of mine, David Sarser, provided some machinery. I asked a customer of mine, Art Ward, to pitch in, and there it was – A&R, which stood for Jack Arnold and Phil Ramone."

Despite the risks involved, Ramone knew that the region's musical activity had been a boon for independents like Regent, Bell, and of course Atlantic. "So many of those midtown studios had been around for a while and had been doing great business," says Ramone. "I figured it was worth a shot."

Like his comrades up the street at Atlantic, Ramone had a combination of recording skill and business savvy that resulted in a staggering flow of business that included the cream of both pop and jazz genres. Ramone's mastery of the echo plate – as heard on tracks like Quincy Jones' 'Soul Bossa Nova,' Van Morrison's 'Brown Eyed Girl,' or Peter, Paul & Mary's 'I Dig Rock and Roll Music' – made A&R one of the most distinctive-sounding facilities in all of New York. Having Jim & Andy's downstairs turned out to be a bonus; Ramone eventually installed a direct line from the control room to the bar in order to alert thirsty session players when it was time to get back behind the baffles.

The studio's popularity led, in 1968, to the opening of a second location, at Columbia's old 799 7th Avenue studio; additional facilities followed. Ramone sold the business in the 1970s, then went on to produce a handful of landmark albums for the likes of Paul Simon, Billy Joel and many others. Today, his shoestring start-up at the corner of 48th and 6th remains his greatest legacy.

SOME NOTABLE RECORDINGS AT A&R

RAY CHARLES
'Let the Good Times Roll'
Recorded June 23rd, 1959

QUINCY JONES
'Soul Bossa Nova'
Recorded September 13th, 1962

ASTRUD GILBERTO WITH STAN GETZ
'The Girl From Ipanema'
Recorded March 19th, 1963

WOODY HERMAN AND HIS ORCHESTRA
'Satin Doll'
Recorded November 22nd, 1963

INTERVIEW PHIL RAMONE

I suppose it didn't hurt to have a name that sounded like you had a direct link to the music industry.

It was a convenient double-entendre [laughs].

What was the room like on 48th?

It was a funny room – fairly dry, though it did have a cement floor – but it was pretty good sized, about 48 by 38 feet. And it sounded great – especially when big groups like the

Tonight Show band with Skitch Henderson started coming in there. We had no air conditioning, no money for that. But we had the chance to get a three-track in there right away; then we went right to four-track as soon as that came out. We became a really good stereo and mono studio – because at that time most people were just making mono records. Stereo was an afterthought.

What were you using for a recorder to start out? Ampex?
Yeah, it was an Ampex 300 three-track and Ampex 350 two-track.

And what were you using for echo early on?
I'd use any kind of room I could find to make a chamber out of, and in this case I used the bathroom. But at the same time I'd befriended a guy who owned this store called Harvey's, and they had an EMT echo plate that they owned that they really hadn't had luck with. So one day I asked if I could use it for a while, just to screw around with it. We put it right in the room and put some straps around it so it wouldn't rattle, and then we took the sides off of it. We tightened it up as best we could so it wouldn't just sound like a boink box. So then we made a deal with Harvey, who let us keep the unit if we let him use our place as a demo studio. A lot of studios just weren't interested in the echo plates – but it was a great space-saver. Not only that, but, believe it or not, that plate with a good tape delay machine really became a big part of the A&R sound.

I believe it. Like Columbia, you obviously placed a premium on quality echo.
True. I loved the Columbia stuff; Fred Plaut was one of my earliest heroes. I was really trying to imitate the sound he was getting over there.

What was the first notable album that came out of A&R?
The Genius of Ray Charles, with Tommy Dowd. Tom just loved it in there, and eventually he started to trust me enough so that I began doing some of the late-night Atlantic dates. These were just incredible R&B recordings.

Can you describe the date you did with the double quartets of Ornette Coleman and Eric Dolphy?
That was a good one! Now you've got to remember, Tom Dowd was probably the most positive person you'd ever meet on the planet – to him, anything was possible. The two groups walk in, Tom sets them up so that they're facing each other, then puts the microphones right between them. We cue up a four-track, and off they go. Now this one

piece they were doing was just going on and on, and it became obvious after a while that they had no intention of ending it anytime soon. Tom and I both looked down at the same time and saw that we had about three minutes of tape left on the four-track reel! Tom looks over at my Ampex and says, "Get the two-track going!" It's a quarter-inch machine, but no matter, we fire it up, Tom starts feeding from the four to the two, just like that, and we just captured the moment. That was what you call flying by the seat of your pants.

You obviously gleaned quite a lot from Dowd during those years.
Tommy was the first guy who really showed me how to use the multi-track. He would capture and isolate these things close enough so you could re-work them. I watched him work the bottom, really refine it. Before that it was difficult to hear. But then as the Beatles and others came along, you really began to have bass definition, to be able to really hear those bass lines. And Tommy really started that.

One of the great recordings from that early period is Getz/Gilberto, which you did with producer Creed Taylor and which got you your first Grammy for Best Engineered Recording.
I remember it well. They all sat in a semi-circle, with the piano at one end and [Joao] Gilberto and Stan [Getz] at the other.

For such a huge hit, 'The Girl From Ipanema' had very humble origins.
Astrud [Gilberto] had been sitting in the control room, and on the second day Norman Gimble happened to walk in with his English lyric to 'Ipanema,' which he'd just written, and handed it to Creed. Creed loved it and said, "You know, we could do this is as a demo for Sarah Vaughan. If we cut it now, I could get it to Quincy tomorrow so Sassy [Vaughan] can cut it." So the recording was really intended to be a demo for another singer.

And the song ends up going Top Five and re-kindling the whole bossa nova trend a whole year later!
Things like that happened a lot back then.

You also had a great team of engineers at A&R during that time.
The engineers who worked there really knew how to capture the room, and you could hear it. Don Frey did some of the biggest commercials of the decade right there – the Yankees theme, ads for Marlboro or Pepsi, things like that. These were huge dates with 45 to 50 people in that room.

What were your microphone preferences back then?

I loved the U47s, of course, but I was also really into the AKG and Sennheiser mics. And the original Sony tube mics, like the C-37, which I used to use on woodwinds quite a bit.

What kind of creative miking techniques did you develop along the way?

I don't know if I created it, but I used to put the trumpets and trombones in a circle with the five saxes surrounding them, right up against the drum kit. I liked the balance of having the miking pattern in 360 – it meant that it didn't splatter. Also, that way I could fit the strings in the room [laughs].

I'd built a booth for the vocals, eventually. The first date I did, it was so ridiculously loud in the vocal mic, I thought, I've gotta do something about this. So I just took two corners of the room and simply put up some pegboard masonite and some fiberglass and created a roof and a window. Everybody else was using stand-up screens, but I didn't like them. I believed in letting the players communicate, so in order for that to happen they had to be able to see each other.

And you weren't using headphones, correct?

No, they were just horrific in those days. They were like those things pilots use to land planes [laughs]. They just didn't work properly. Sometimes the singers would use headphones, but even then I preferred using these little KLH 8-inch speakers on a mic stand, flip them out of phase and put them right behind the condenser mic. You could come up with enough level using those speakers, at least to the point where the singers could certainly hear the rhythm section being fed to them.

What else contributed to the sound of A&R?

We had to build things that were typical of A&R and not typical of regular consoles. We didn't have a lot of money, and I'd keep putting the money into the pre-amps and special EQs. I always felt that if you recorded the room with the right mic and you had the right blend of leakage and presence, you could create incredible echoes. That's why I kept all the chambers separated. And the minute I had an extra few bucks, I went out and bought yet another chamber. We just didn't have the physical room for real live chambers. Eventually we rented more space in the building and hung those in the back with the tape library! When you don't have money, you'd be amazed at what you can do!

In many ways, that seemed to be an advantage – you had to rely on ingenuity.

Absolutely.

It must have been satisfying when you got to open a second location at
Columbia's former studios at 799 7th Avenue.
Eventually it got to the point where Creed Taylor, who I just loved working with, told me,
"I can't compete with the clients you've got." Because at that point we only had one main
room – we had a Studio B for vocals, but that was it. So Creed finally moved over to New
Jersey where he could operate normal hours, start in the morning and be done by 5pm. At
A&R we were getting commercials, film scores, all this other work. So we desperately
needed another location. I would have dedicated one room totally for Creed – all of the
Verve stuff was just amazing. How else could I have recorded artists like J.J. [Johnson] and
Kai [Winding], Wes Montgomery, and people like that? But it was obvious that we really
needed another space, and then Columbia's space became available.

You were a big fan of the Columbia sound – what was it like walking in there after
buying the building from them?
When we got there they'd torn every wire out of the place, left us with nothing. But that
place had this great staircase that went up seven floors that they'd been using for echo,
and that sounded great. Then I found these cement rooms down in the basement and
reactivated them all. That's where I put the EMTs – four per room, suspended in there like
in a meat locker.

You had the EMTs in rooms that were like chambers?
It was just a way of keeping them properly isolated – we didn't use the rooms as
chambers, per se. By then we knew the EMTs worked great and we'd learned the right
way to use them. In fact, early on when I wasn't making any money, I actually hired myself
out to tune people's EMT chambers. For a while there it became my secret weapon – I
even told people that they couldn't watch me while I was doing the job. You know, "Just
get me a half-dozen extra springs and don't talk to me." [laughs.] People were fascinated.

There's enough water under the bridge – what was your secret?
Well, part of it was that I tuned them so you couldn't change the lengths – and that they
were individually set for rhythm, strings, horns, vocals. We had the four dedicated
chambers. That's why, when you hear some of the earlier A&R things like Quincy Jones'
Big Band Bossa Nova or any of the Count Basie material ...

... they have a real identifiable sound.
The other thing is that we'd refurbished the floor so that it was cement/vermiculite, this

battleship gray color. It was pretty dry, but reflective enough to have plenty of life. Which meant that on those kinds of records, the brass or the bass wouldn't run on it, and it had a really nice sound for the players.

By the early 1970s you'd moved again.

When the wrecking ball hit 112 West 48th, we still had tons of business, so we found this other spot in the Leeds Music Building at 322 West 48th Street, and refurbished it from top to bottom. We became partial owners and had the first and second floors, which were R1 and R2, plus the basement. So we called the two different studios the A building and the R building.

Looking back, how does A&R compare to the sophisticated studios you've occupied over the years?

A&R was so non-acoustically-correct, at least compared to the way studios have been constructed for the last 35 years. You get inside these places now and they're like castles, and yet so often the players aren't able to look at each or hear each other. There should just be your comfort zone, that's all. I want the players to feel as if they were performing in a nightclub.

That's what I did with Sinatra in the 1990s – I took him out of the booth, put him in the middle of the band on a small stage and let him use a small wireless hand mic. Not the way most people would work, but I didn't think it was so far out. Come to think of it, neither did Frank!

THE MAKING OF *GETZ/GILBERTO*

On a cold New York morning in February 1962, producer Creed Taylor and saxophonist Stan Getz hopped on a shuttle down to Washington. They were heading for an afternoon recording session with guitarist Charlie Byrd, who was just back from a tour of Brazil and armed with a cache of exotic new songs by composer Antonio Carlos "Tom" Jobim, leader of "bossa nova," Rio de Janeiro's nascent musical movement.

"The performances weren't as loose as they could have been," recalls Taylor, "mostly because there weren't any Brazilians involved. Still, I thought the tunes were incredibly catchy. Most of all, it opened up the door for this wave of Brazilian talent."

Released that fall, *Jazz Samba* – recorded with two mics using a 7½ ips Sony tape machine – became an immediate hit. It featured a Top 20 single in 'Desafinado' and touched off a US bossa nova craze that the following year spawned a parade of fad singles, including Elvis Presley's 'Bossa Nova Baby' and Eydie Gorme's 'Blame it On the

Bossa Nova'. Taylor, however, was determined to keep the music on a respectable path. An initial studio meeting with Jobim (an adept pianist and guitarist) resulted in the successful debut *Jobim, The Composer of Desafinado, Plays*. Suitably impressed, Jobim rang up colleague João Gilberto – the man credited with inventing the bossa-nova guitar style – and implored him to come to New York for a Carnegie Hall performance followed by a recording date with saxophonist Getz and percussionist Milton Banana at A&R Studios on 48th Street.

As Taylor recalls, the relaxed and productive nature of the March 1963 sessions for the now-legendary *Getz/Gilberto* album (expertly engineered by A&R's Phil Ramone) was due mainly to the laid-back manner of Jobim, whose piano colorations (and original songs) propelled the recordings.

> "THE LP ALMOST DIDN'T HAPPEN. A KNOWN RECLUSE, GILBERTO MADE THE NYC TRIP WITH NO APPARENT INTENTION TO LEAVE HIS HOTEL."

"The room we used at A&R was a small, dead space, with headsets for the reverb. There was nothing spectacular about it at all," says Taylor. "But Jobim was like this bubbling kid, bursting with enthusiasm. He was all music – he couldn't have been less interested in the technical side of things. Generally he'd get it in one or two takes – and since Getz worked the same way, it was a good fit. But what was most remarkable was the sound coming from Gilberto's guitar, which was not so easy to capture, and the expression from Jobim's piano playing. He always reminded me of Bill Evans in that way – less is more, that approach."

Ironically, the album that would ultimately score a handful of Grammys almost didn't happen. A known recluse, Gilberto had made the Big Apple trip, along with his wife Astrud, with no apparent intention of leaving the hotel. It would take some quick diplomacy on the part of Getz's wife Monica to help keep history on track.

"Monica went over to the hotel where the Gilbertos were staying, got them into a cab and brought them over to 48th Street," says Taylor. "Here was this guy, who'd been used to playing in a quiet Rio environment, suddenly thrust into big New York City. Those Brazilians on that first tour were anything but overt, but he was probably the most reclusive of all."

Astrud's decision to join her husband on the trip to New York would have life-changing implications. One of the designated tracks was a melodic new Jobim number entitled 'Garota de Ipanema,' its lyric inspired by the real-life adventures of one Helo Pinheiro, a captivating (and, apparently, 14-year-old) female beach-goer from Rio. On a lark, Astrud was persuaded to sing the English lyric to the song, ostensibly to be used as a demo. Ramone hung a U47 in front of Astrud – an untrained vocalist who'd never sung a note on tape – and five minutes later, 'The Girl From Ipanema' was complete.

"She could speak English and she had that little accent," recalls Taylor. "It worked."

That same week, the wildly popular *Jazz Samba* capped a seven-month chart climb, becoming the first jazz album in history to reach Number One. Not wishing to slow the momentum with yet another album of Brazilian music, Verve tossed the *Getz/Gilberto* master on to the shelf, where it sat for the better part of a year. By the time Getz finally convinced the label to release the album the following spring, the Beatles had conquered the world, and bossa nova was, for all intents and purposes, history.

It might have been the beginning and end of Astrud's career as a recording artist, had it not been for a small jazz station broadcasting out of Columbus, Ohio, that began regularly airing 'The Girl from Ipanema' in the wake of the March 1964 release of *Getz/Gilberto*. "This one particular jockey got into that song," remembers Taylor, "and just banged away at it; the requests started coming in – and suddenly, we started seeing sales. I remember asking, 'What's going on with this "Girl from Ipanema"?' That's really how it began, just like that."

Verve judiciously whittled 'Ipanema' down to a three-minute single; by August, the song was at Number Five, re-igniting the bossa craze and lighting a fire under *Getz/Gilberto*, which climbed all the way to Number Two and remained on the chart for two years. Jobim's economical arrangements and Getz's pulsating sax added a sophisticated air to Jobim staples like 'Doralice,' 'Desafinado' and 'Corcovado,' each one featuring the sinuous vocalizing and guitar elegance of João Gilberto (whose opening scat on 'Ipanema' remains one of the most goosebump-inducing moments in recorded history).

After appearing on two of the biggest jazz albums to date, Getz eventually shook off the samba in favor of more traditional surroundings. He died in 1991. Jobim spent the next few decades working in a considerably more complex style, with equally satisfying results. Astrud's five minutes of session work (without compensation) sparked a career that has continued on-and-off for five decades (she recently resurfaced with her newest release, *Jungle*). Meanwhile, Taylor would go on to achieve many more successes for Verve as well as his own label, CTI, recording venerable acts such as Freddie Hubbard, Stanley Turrentine, George Benson and Hubert Laws. Nearly 40 years later, *Getz/Gilberto* remains Taylor's single greatest achievement as a producer.

kirshner's kids

smiths Carole King and Paul Simon recording demos as The Cosines (with Gerry Goffin behind), RCA 'A', late 1958.

In the super-charged atmosphere of New York circa 1960, young bucks roamed the streets just north of Times Square, looking for a piece of the action. Times have changed. Today, upstart artists regularly wade through a sea of lawyers, managers, binders, and red tape in order to secure a record deal. Forty-five years ago, if you were young, musical, and a New Yorker, very often all it took was a knock on the right door.

"When I was 13 years old, I was going to the Rhodes School on 54th Street," says noted composer/arranger Artie Butler. "One day I was walking back to the subway and I happened to go past this building that said 'King Records,' and so I went down the stairs and into the office, announced that I was a rock'n'roll singer from Brooklyn and that I'd like to make a record. This little white kid, walking into King Records, of all places! Can you imagine?

"The guy who I was talking to turned out to be Henry Glover [a musician, arranger and producer with King]. And he says, 'OK, let me hear you, kid.' So I go over to this upright piano and start banging away, and he says, 'Hey, you can sing and you can play!' And so he signs me to a contract – to make one record – for the Deluxe label, which was their subsidiary. I just recently found a copy of the record, which they'd pressed up as both a 45 and a 78. It was called 'Lock, Stock and Barrel.'

"Henry produced it, we cut it at Beltone Studios, a small studio that was further downtown, away from most of the other places. The drummer on the date turned out to be none other than Sonny Greer – from the Duke Ellington Orchestra! He shows up with his set of 20 drums like he used to have, but the best part was that he couldn't cut the triplets! He was a jazz drummer: it just wasn't in his bag of chops. But there it was – 13 years old, my first date ever in a studio, with the great Henry Glover producing and Sonny Greer drumming. Can you believe it?

"But that's part of what that era was all about – so much music happening in one place at one time. And it'll never happen like that ever again."

During 1958, rock'n'roll continued to plow across the country, sending sales of 45s into uncharted territory. Its impact was particularly noticeable across the East River in the borough of Brooklyn, a ten-minute subway ride from midtown Manhattan. A soulful community, teeming with arcades, pizzerias, and corner stores, Brooklyn oozed musicality. In 1958, baseball's original heartbreak kids, the Brooklyn Dodgers, abruptly packed their bags and moved out to Los Angeles, the cultural antithesis of New York, sending long-suffering Brooklynites into a tailspin. A handful of teenaged Brooklynites attempted to fill the void by making music – and, in the process, began building an empire from scratch.

Their salvation was an enterprising businessman named Don Kirshner, a local jingle writer down on his luck and looking for action. Sensing the commercial viability of the burgeoning pop movement, Kirshner joined forces in 1958 with another Brooklyn-based entrepreneur, Al Nevins, and launched a publishing company, Aldon Music. Rather than scout out here-today-gone-tomorrow teen singing stars, Kirshner went straight to the source, by recruiting some of the region's best young songwriting talent. At the start of the 1960s, Kirshner and Nevins moved to 1650 Broadway – the heart of Manhattan's hitsville – taking with them a posse that included Barry Mann, Brooks Arthur, Gerry Goffin and a 17-year-old secretary named Carole Klein, who aspired to record her own songs under the name of Carole King. Most of Kirshner's kids hailed from Brooklyn; all were Jewish.

"They say it was the water, but who knows," reflects producer/engineer Brooks Arthur, more than 40 years on. "Maybe it was the latkes."

BROOKLYN INVASION

The Brooklyn invasion had its roots in the vaudeville era of early 20th century New York, a byproduct of Eastern European and Russian Jewish immigrants finding their voice in the new world. Responding to the demand for short, catchy tunes for Broadway shows and the radio market, composers like George and Ira Gershwin, Jerome Kern, Irving Berlin, and Sammy Cahn quickly established themselves in New York and later around the world. Their unbridled success became a clarion call to thousands of other aspiring young writers who launched New York's formidable songwriting establishment from inside the cramped offices along New York's East 14th Street, otherwise known as Tin Pan Alley. By the 1950s, the action had moved uptown, and was centered in and around the Brill Building, located at 1619 Broadway.

The young wannabes who filed into Kirshner's tiny cubicles each day were, in many ways, remarkably different from their song-plugging predecessors. For the first time, young people comprised the majority of the record-buying public. Songs that dealt specifically with youth issues – break ups, nagging parents, school problems – were in constant demand. "And who could write songs about young people better than young people?" observes Tom Dowd. "Kirshner's writers had their finger on the pulse."

"We went against the grain," notes Artie Butler. "The generation that preceded us were strictly professionals, did everything by the book. Whereas for many in my generation, it was 101 percent passion – we didn't know anything else. It was never a 'job.' For a lot of us, it was escaping. Many of the guys I knew didn't have such great childhoods; the music was our enchanted forest."

"The Brill Building in 1960," recalls Butler, "had the Turf restaurant on one side,

Jack Dempsey's restaurant on the other. Big meeting places for musicians, A&R guys, everybody. There were tons of music publishers in the area as well. And, beginning with the rock'n'roll era, a lot of recording studios. That was no accident."

Only a few hot dog stands separated the major players, among them Dick Charles Studio, at 729 7th Avenue near the corner of West 48th; Associated, just a few doors down at 723 7th Avenue; and, one block south, Mira Sound, located on the ground floor of the Hotel America at 145-155 West 47th Street. Over the next 10 years, these studios, along with neighboring A&R on 48th, Columbia's 799 7th and, six blocks north, Bell Sound on West 54th, would produce some of the most enduring tracks in the annals of popular music.

HOUSEWIFE SUPERSTAR

At the start of the 1960s, no one captured New York's anything-can-happen mentality better than Florence Greenberg, of Passaic, New Jersey, a housewife-turned-record mogul whose rise to power defies basic business logic. With her children grown and in need of a career, Greenberg accepted an offer to do volunteer work at a midtown publisher's office. She became intrigued with the machinations of the record business, and, almost overnight, began thinking about launching her own record label.

Back in Passaic, Greenberg got wind of a local teen singing group who wrote their own songs and performed frequently in the area. She saw the all-girl quartet as her ticket to hitsville, and in 1958 asked the group, known as The Shirelles, to become the first artists on her newly established Tiara label.

'I Met Him on a Sunday' – recorded at Beltone Studios – made waves locally, but Greenberg had bigger game in mind. In 1959, securing office space along Broadway's packed 1600 block, She hung out her shingle as owner-operator of Scepter Records (later spinning off a subsidiary, Wand). In the meantime, The Shirelles were gradually making gains on the New York music scene, but still needed a bona fide hit. Kirshner rang up his husband-and-wife team, Gerry Goffin and Carole King, themselves still on the lookout for a first smash. In January 1961, the Goffin-King song 'Will You Love Me Tomorrow' reached Number One, giving The Shirelles their national breakout and Greenberg a place among Manhattan's record-making elite. It would be a role she would never relinquish.

The site of Greenberg's early-1960s conquests was Bell Sound Recording Studios, located at 237 West 54th Street and operated by partners Al Weintraub and Dan Cronin. During the 1950s, Bell had churned out its share of pop and jazz staples. In November 1955, a barely teenaged Frankie Lymon and The Teenagers cut the million seller, 'Why

Do Fools Fall In Love,' from Bell's Studio A. Jazz artists, ranging from Dinah Washington to Duke Ellington, frequently made use of Bell's spacious facilities. Even country popsters The Everly Brothers made the trek all the way from Nashville to record their 1959 crooner classic, 'Let it Be Me.'

That same year, the teenage Artie Butler got his first taste of the pro-studio environment, when he was offered a job assisting the technical hands inside Bell's main control room.

"I'd always wanted to be around the music business," recalls Butler, "so when I was 16 I got a job working in the record department of a store called Corvette's. At night, I was playing piano in a club called Ben Maxie's Town and Country, a really nice place that used to book these great acts like Martin & Lewis. This guy used to come into the record store looking for different songs, and by then I'd become pretty knowledgeable. So after a while he asked me if I'd like a job working in a recording studio. I said, 'I'd love it!' This guy turned out to be Abe Steinberg, who was a cutter – he

> "FLORENCE GREENBERG DID SOME VOLUNTARY WORK AT AN NYC MUSIC PUBLISHER, BECAME INTRIGUED, AND BEGAN PLANS TO LAUNCH HER OWN RECORD LABEL."

made acetates and did the mastering. He brought me over to Bell Sound and gave me a job as what they used to call the 'button pusher,' because back then they didn't have machines that would automatically start, you'd have to close the heads and push the button to get it going. As button pusher, I also had to set up and break down the studio, clean the mic cables, and do other chores like that."

Having the opportunity to cut records was the perfect excuse to cut classes; like many of the best sound crafters in the business, Butler never found time for a formal education. "I dropped out of high school, which my parents were none too thrilled about," says Butler. "But I had no regrets. It was an apprenticeship par excellence.

"When you walked into Bell, you took an elevator to the second floor to get to Studio B and C," remembers Butler. "Studio B was smaller; it could handle around 15 to 18 people or so. I remember recording the Duke Ellington band in there. Studio C was strictly for vocals, narration and things like that. Agencies used it a lot for commercials. The cutting rooms, mastering rooms, tape library and so forth were situated around the perimeter of the studio.

"On the top floor was Studio A, the big room, which was about 30 by 60 feet, with ceilings that were about 20 to 22 feet high," says Butler. "When I got there they were using a Westex console with these big fat rotary faders. And all the floors in between had music copyists and other businesses, because Bell didn't take up the entire building."

GOLDEN MOMENTS

For Butler, a skilled pianist with high musical aspirations, Bell was a gift, a first-class finishing school as well as a pipeline to Manhattan's musical elite. "I got to meet the greatest musicians in New York at that time," says Butler. "Pop, R&B, country records, you name it. Because I could play piano, I used to set up the studio early, then go over to the piano and play for a bit. Sometimes the guys on the session would be coming in and they'd be, 'Wow, you can play!' One time, the granddaddy of all jazz bassists, Milt Hinton, came in, heard me playing, and told me he was coming back the next evening an hour before his scheduled session so he could play with me! This guy was unreal, I'd known about him for years, and there we were playing in the studio together. After that he invites me out to his house to meet Count Basie – there I am, schlepping out on the subway, 16 years old, to meet the Count. This sort of thing was happening all the time, just because of the incredible amount of talent that was coming in and out of that studio during those years."

As Butler recalls, Bell had its share of golden moments, not all of them purely musical. "Dinah Washington had just signed with Roulette Records, and it was her very first session at Bell with the new label," recalls Butler. "It was a large orchestra session. Now Dinah had her own way of doing things – she'd always come in after everyone was rehearsed, so the band would be sitting there waiting for her to show up. But she was selling so many records, it didn't matter – you had to work with her.

"So on this particular date the door flies open and she yells out, 'Do not fear, Queenie's here.' She walks in wearing this outrageous fur coat with a white fur hat with flowers, turns to her producer, Henry Glover, and says, 'Glover, you're getting two tracks of each. That's it.' So they're starting this first number with the orchestra playing live right behind her, when suddenly she looks over to the string section, and there's this guy

■ **MARSHALL CRENSHAW (musician)** "You take a place like Bell Sound, and you listen to the Dionne Warwick records or Little Anthony and The Imperials records … there's not a whole lot of isolation going on, it was large enough so that you could really spread people around. So what you're hearing is the air moving around in the room, and it really gives the records that sense of immediacy, that sense of time and place. Because you can just hear the room."

in the front row wearing these salmon-colored pants. She stops the orchestra and says, 'What the hell kind of stupid-ass pants are those? Either he takes them off or I'm not singing.' Now it took this guy 30 years to get to the front row and there's no way he's moving to the back row for anything. So he takes his pants off and played in his underwear! And after 10 minutes of laughter they resumed the take."

A chance meeting with kingpin writer-producers Jerry Leiber and Mike Stoller became a major turning point for Butler. "They'd come in to do a session, and whoever it was they'd had on piano that day couldn't really cut the part," recalls Butler. "They had this 30-piece orchestra in there, the clock was ticking, there was a lot of pressure to get it done without going into overtime, of course. I stuck my head out of the control room and said, 'You know, Mr. Leiber, I can play that part.' And he looks at me like I'd just got off a rocket ship from Pluto. He says, 'Are you sure?' You know, ignorance is bliss, and being young is another excuse for ignorance.

"So after they let the orchestra go, I figured out how long it would take me to run from the control room out to the piano, made a mark on the tape that allowed me an extra eight bars or so, then set up an open record track. I ran in there, and when the passage came around I played it, ran back in, and turned off the machine. Then I put my hands out as if to say, 'Voila!' I ran back the tape, and when it came to the passage I went to the console, rolled off the other guy's part and pulled up mine. They were just thrilled – they gave me a hug and in the same breath said, 'Will you come work for us?' As soon as I'd trained a new person to take my place at Bell, I began working for Leiber & Stoller. And that's literally how I got started as a player."

In Dan Cronin, Bell had an astute manager who kept the studio in step with the latest trends in record-making technology. By the early 1960s Bell already had an eight-track in house, to go with a generous supply of Telefunken microphones and transparent, hand-built consoles. Despite its technical superiority, it was Studio A's spacious recording room and superb echo chamber (one of the best live rooms in town) that gave Bell its signature sound.

mira stars

Inspired by Florence Greenberg's phenomenal success with The Shirelles, an army of record producers began hastily assembling tracks around their own all-girl vocal acts. Nearly 450 different girl groups would bombard the charts through 1966, but the peak period of activity came between 1962 and 1964, as hitmakers like The Cookies, The Crystals, The Paris Sisters, Little Eva, The Chiffons, and The Dixie Cups provided regular pay-checks for Brill contributors Gerry Goffin and Carole King ('The Locomotion'), Barry Mann and his wife Cynthia Weil ('I Love How You Love Me'), and many others.

The label that reaped the biggest return was Red Bird Records, launched in early 1964 by Leiber & Stoller in conjunction with local impresario George Goldner. Songwriting spouses Jeff Barry and Ellie Greenwich, authors of many girl-group hits and near-misses during the previous year, were retained as Red Bird's composing/producing brains trust. They immediately rewarded their new employers with a Number One smash, The Dixie Cups' 'Chapel of Love.'

"When I left Bell Sound Studios to work for Leiber and Stoller, I met Jeff and Ellie, who were writers signed to Trio Music, their publishing firm," says Artie Butler. "They

> "THOSE SHANGRI-LAS TRACKS MADE AT MIRA, WITH GEORGE 'SHADOW' MORTON PRODUCING AND BROOKS ARTHUR ENGINEERING, WERE JUST BEAUTIFUL."

were writing hit songs and making hit records, and I became their arranger and pianist on many of them. Ellie sang backup on many of the records as well. She had a great sound and really good musical instincts.

"Jeff was great in the control room," says Butler. "He always knew exactly what he wanted to hear, which made it easy for the arranger and the musicians. There were so many times I walked out of a session we'd just finished and I couldn't stop singing the song we'd just recorded. That was Jeff's secret weapon: he really knew how to write songs people would remember."

Red Bird's studio of choice was Mira Sound, located on the main floor of the dingy Hotel America on 145 West 47th Street, a short walk from 7th Avenue and the bright lights of Times Square. During the 1950s and 1960s the hotel itself was still active; in 1959, comic Lenny Bruce, an America regular, taped his lunatic 'Captain Whackencracker' from a third-floor guest room. "This place was not to be believed," says engineer Brooks Arthur, another key member of the Red Bird team. "At one time it had been quite an elegant hotel, but it was hardly that by the time I got there. The studio had not been maintained exceptionally well, but the room had a definite sound, and some of the sonic peculiarities of the room actually *contributed* to the sound. The control room was where the kitchen used to be, roughly where the stoves were, and the studio may have been where they prepared the food, or the actual dining room itself. With the ceiling as high as it was, it most likely was the dining room."

Red Bird's next – and most celebrated – success came by way of an outsider: George "Shadow" Morton, a Brooklyn-born, Long Island-based freelance songwriter and producer. Morton told producer Barry that not only did he have a hit record up his sleeve, he also had the perfect girl-group to record it. In fact, he had neither, but when Barry called his bluff, Morton was forced to take action.

Quickly, Morton tracked down a teenaged quartet from Queens, consisting of sisters Mary and Betty Weiss and twins Marge and Mary Ann Ganser. The group, known as The Shangri-Las, agreed to let Morton produce a demo on their behalf at Ultrasonic, a small demo studio in Long Island. On the way to the session, Morton, still a man without a song, jerked the car to the side of the road and scribbled down the foundation for what would become a girl-group magnum opus. 'Remember (Walkin' In The Sand),' would eventually be a Top Five smash.

LEADERS OF THE PACK

The Shangri-Las were quite unlike any other female act of their era. Tough, hip and streetwise, the group – in particular, lead singer Mary Weiss – exuded a sense of urgency often missing from cookie-cutter girl-group efforts. "They were real, no doubt," remarked Jerry Leiber. "Just like their producer."

"Those tracks at Mira Sound, with George producing and Brooks Arthur engineering, were just beautiful," says Butler. "George knew exactly what he wanted to hear in the control room. The rhythm tracks would be made in advance; the background singers would be grouped around one mic, and lead singer Mary would be right next to them on her own mic separated by a see-through baffle. Occasionally they'd do the backgrounds as an overdub."

"Artie Butler was my connection to the musicians," notes Morton. "Artie was credited as 'arranger.' He would write down on a piece of paper all the ideas I had for the music. He had that talent. I did not. He could write anything down on staff paper [music manuscript]. I would sing him a part and he would always have something to add. And it was always great. You know, you have to let the musicians know that you're open to suggestions – that they have something valuable. I would listen. I had great musicians on the sessions, all due to Butler. He could translate me and get the best players to reproduce his arrangements. I didn't know how to deal with musicians … I can't play anything. In fact, if you remember, I'm the new kid on the block – I dunno nothin'! I got into this business as a joke!"

Capitalizing on the group's tough-chick image, Morton and crew reconvened inside Mira Sound a short time later and cut 'Leader of the Pack,' a teenage mini-opera featuring another heart-shredding Mary Weiss vocal and, to really drive the point home, the sound of a motorcycle failing to negotiate a sharp turn (provided by an actual Harley being revved up outside the hotel's front lobby). The combination of music and mayhem was enough to put The Shangri-Las on top of the Hot 100 in Thanksgiving week 1964.

"The group that, for me, really signifies that entire period was The Shangri-Las," says Butler. "They were the bad girls. They weren't the romantic types, they were the step-out, juvenile delinquents. And like everyone else, all the guys down at the studio had a huge crush on Mary Weiss. I'll always remember watching Mary doing her vocal overdub during the recording of 'Walkin' in the Sand.' Our tongues were hanging out, she was so freakin' sexy. Long straight blonde hair, the ultimate shiksa goddess."

In the fickle world of pop, fortunes can change in the blink of an eye. By the middle of 1965, the girl-group phenomenon had all but vanished, pushed aside by the trebly guitars and thick British harmonies of the post-Beatles invasion.

"When these English groups started coming in," says Artie Butler, "it was a definite sound, and obviously it had a pronounced affect on the creative element in New York and elsewhere. In 1963, guys like Neil Sedaka and Howie Greenfield were on top of the world. But as the bands got smaller and became self-contained, the entire recording industry became smaller as well. It changed everything. There were still singers who didn't write, and that went on a little longer. In the old days we used to have songwriters walking in all the time. But then that too became a thing of the past.

"I vividly remember sitting in someone's office when this young songwriter walked in with some material, and the secretary told him, 'I'm sorry, we don't accept outside material.' As a result of that new way of thinking, I'm willing to bet that on countless occasions, some publishers lost a great song.

"About two years ago on a Sunday I went back over to the building, I wanted to show

■ **GERRY GOFFIN (songwriter)** **"The Beatles, Bob Dylan, the Rolling Stones, the British invasion. All of a sudden, artists were writing their own music, and it was different. After Carole and I first went to see Bob Dylan at Carnegie Hall in 1961, we took all our old demos and broke them in half. We said, 'We have to grow up.'"**

my fiancé what the Brill Building looked like. The building was closed, and in the lobby there was a security guy there, who wouldn't even let me take a picture. I said, 'You've gotta be kidding.' I said, 'I used to work in this building, I made records here.' He was this stupid young guy who just wouldn't budge. So I ended up with a picture of me standing outside the building in the freezing cold. But nevertheless, I have the greatest memories of that place and everything that surrounded it."

INTERVIEW **BROOKS ARTHUR**

During the early 1960s, the trio of studios that occupied a single city block along 7th Avenue between West 47th and West 48th – Dick Charles, Associated and Mira Sound – became, for all intents and purposes, girl-group central. It was there that Brooks Arthur, an aspiring singer and songwriter, turned his attention to engineering, in the process becoming the chief architect of New York's girl-group sound.

How did you get started?

As a child, I took weekly singing lessons and performed every chance I got. It was not easy for my parents, who owned a candy store, to afford those lessons – but they made sure that I had them. My Bar Mitzvah gift was a Revere tape recorder, and I would attach alligator clips to the speakers behind the TV and radio to record my favorite shows and singers.

I entered the music business through a part-time high school job, working in the mailroom at Decca Records in New York. My take-home pay was $26.04 per week. The greatest job in the world. One day, while I was delivering mail to Milt Gabler at Decca, he invited me to sit in and observe a session at their 50 West 57th Street tenth floor studio, and that session was the great Ella Fitzgerald recording to a stunning arrangement by the incomparable Gordon Jenkins.

I was hooked. Two years later, I began working at Kapp Records, where I assisted Michael Kapp in the A&R Department and at their in-house studio, which had Ampex recording equipment. I would observe Mickey Kapp doing great quarter-inch edits and reel-to-reel safety copies for their library.

In 1961, I arrived at Aldon, with people like Jack Keller, Artie Kaplan, Barry Mann and all the other Brooklyn writers. I was singing demos and writing songs at the same time. As a singer I was fantastic – as a songwriter I was good. When Don Kirshner would be pitching songs at the meetings, there'd always be songs by Carole King and Gerry Goffin, Sedaka-Greenfield, Mann-Weil. There was so much incredible talent in those writers' cubicles. So while I was doing these demos, I started hanging out in the control room at

Dick Charles, 729 7th Avenue. When I got there, Dick Charles noticed my interest in the board and the equipment.

One day, he turned to me and said, "Do you like engineering?" I said, "Yes." He said, "Try to bring in some of the Aldon account and I'll teach you how to engineer the demos." I asked Al Nevins and Don Kirshner [Aldon Music] and the other writers if they would take a chance with mixing their demos at Dick Charles' studio. My songwriter friends were fiercely loyal and agreed … and I got the job.

Though it was essentially a demo studio, the name Dick Charles pops up quite a bit in New York folklore – Neil Diamond even cut his first hit there.
It was a tiny studio with two big old mono Ampex tape machines with a single VU, and a console with Daven rotary pots that switched from 'A' to 'B' – which meant from one mono machine to the other: hence the expression "mono-to-mono." You'd add different layers with each overdub and generation. For mics, they had those bulletproof Shure SM-58s, EV RE-20s, real workhorse models, and a couple of tube U-47s for vocalists and other solo instruments … and of course, hand claps.

Eventually you started working over at Associated, right next door at 723 7th.
Associated was a really good studio. It had two rooms. Studio A was a decent size room with 14-foot ceilings, B was smaller, an overdub or piano room. We did a lot of the full-production Carole King and Barry Mann demos in there, or sometimes they'd just use B and make a piano-vocal demo. Their songs were so good, their piano playing was so captivating, they could sell them just like that with a simple p/v [piano/vocal] demo. Studio A had a lot of ambience, but of course you'd lose the ambience when you'd go over to B to do the backing vocals. But we'd rectify that by using the chamber.

What was their chamber like?
At Associated we had a stairwell that we'd use for echo – except that it was *outside* the building! It was the fire-escape stairwell; it faced 48th Street. If you were walking past the Metropole on 7th and you took a left onto 48th on your way to Manny's, you'd see that stairwell coming off the building about a quarter of the way down. It was like one of those old movie theater stairwells, except that it was this cavernous, cemented thing with metal steps. And I used that as a live chamber. We also had an old Fisher springbox unit that we'd use more often than the live chamber, because we'd pick up too many fire engines and police car sirens from the exterior chamber. I affectionately refer to it as the 'Boing' box.

Are there any records in particular that stand out from the Associated period?

Yes, three. The Raindrops' record of 'What A Guy' – which was really Jeff and Ellie – was made in Studio A, mono to mono to mono. I was using a Fairchild compressor in order to keep the levels uniform between the machines and to try not to get too much loss through the generations. It was on that session that I started using the mic that would become my secret weapon: an old Altec 633A, the 'salt shaker.'

That mic would follow me through the years to at least four different studios. I'd put it underneath the snare drum, pointed straight up, in order to catch a bit of the snare rattle. Even as I began using more sophisticated mics on the top – Sennheisers, even a Neumann on occasion – I'd still have the Altec underneath. The other two records that stand out are 'My Boyfriend's Back' by The Angels and 'Hang On, Sloopy' by The McCoys.

Can you trace the origins of the girl-group studio sound and how you made it happen?

'My Boyfriend's Back,' which was cut at Associated, really crystallized the whole genre – it had the handclaps, the dialogue, it was the springboard to groups like The Shangri-Las. One of the big ingredients was doubling and tripling the backing vocals. Keep in mind that we're dealing with mono to mono to mono only … we're talking some serious generational loss! I'd make up for it by EQ-ing the tracks through a Pultec EQP1A or compressing it with my Fairchilds or another Altec mono compressor.

"Another thing I figured out was moving the girls to a different position around the mic for each overdub track, so that the mic would be picking up a different 'voicegram:' same singers, but the new placement would really make it sound fuller. Once I honed the sound, I tried not to deviate from it. That formula remained a constant for me through the years.

Those records really have a 'New York' feel to them – a lot of atmosphere, a lot of unusual sounds.

All the kids and the singers had studio attitude. Jeff Barry was really inventive – he liked those little "street sounds." Like The Dixie Cups records – 'Iko Iko,' for instance – those clanging noises are ashtrays that were sitting on the control-room windowsill.

I remember the drum sound we got at Associated. It was always freezing in there in the winter and they had this big old electric heater that you'd plug in. Someone like Buddy Salzman or Al Rogers would turn the thing over and we'd use that with brushes as a snare sound. Or a garbage can. We were always looking for something different. Jeff was always searching for drum 'combos' – and when they worked, the sound was undeniable. With his OK, I'd reuse those ideas with other acts and producers.

What brought you over to Mira Sound?

I think I got a call from Carole [King] or Gerry [Goffin], who were working on 'Hey, Girl' with Freddie Scott. Bill McMeekin, who was a great engineer, happened to be under the weather that day and so they asked me to come in and pinch-hit. Here was this great pro studio where they cut master recordings – they even had a three-track Ampex that enabled me to use tape echo on the snare for that song – ta-ta-ta-ta-, ta-ta-ta-ta – which worked really nicely.

"I helped them finish that cut and the rest of Freddie's album, and I became instant friends with the studio owner, Bob Goldman, who invited me to come over to work as an independent engineer. I gave my notice at Associated, and suddenly I was at Mira working on a commission basis and having to bring in my own clients. It was a real opportunity to work in a great place. I was so thankful to be there.

What was Mira like?

The walls of the studio were lined with these egg-crate panels, which absorbed the sound nicely. The drums were against the back wall facing toward the control room; to the drummer's left was the bass, and to his left was the piano, facing towards the drummer. The guitars were in front of the drum kit facing me, the percussion was to the right of the piano along one wall, and then there were two pillars on the left side of the room, around which we strategically situated strings and/or horns – they were alcoves, remainders of the old dining-room configuration.

The horns were closer to the drum kits and the strings were closer to the control room in order to avoid leakage problems. We used these big multi-colored gobos that were about six to eight feet high to further delineate those sections, and used smaller clam-shaped dividers for the guitars. The gobos were small enough so that the guitar players could see over them, follow the arranger or conductor, and further see into the control room. Everyone had a bird's eye view of the conductor except for the piano player. I had a pretty great view of it all.

For the vocalists, we had two 'houses' [vocal booths on wheels]. One house was for the backgrounds, one house was for the lead vocalist. We'd isolate the vocalists during the live sessions, and when the session was over and it was time to overdub the voices, we'd pull them out of the houses and build a three-gobo room separator about ten feet from the control room. That way, we could utilize the height of the ceiling, the sound of the room, and even the vocal deflection off of the control room window, plus a great microphone, yielding the 'Mira Sound vocal sound.'

In the control room at Mira they had a board with Langevin slide faders, like 24 or 30 of them. They were phenomenal … smooth as silk … the Rolls Royce of faders. They slowly became an extension of my fingers and I played those faders like a great piano player plays a keyboard. There was a rack of Pultecs, some Lang equalizers, and some high-level mixers so that I could sub-group my strings and/or horns and then bring them back onto the board using just one or two faders.

Because we had a lot of stuff going – drums, bass, guitars, vocals, backgrounds, percussion – I could make live mixes on the spot, to mono, two-track and three-track, all Ampex. Later we got a four-track, the 300 series. I owe a lot of the success to my sound and mixes to two of the greatest assistant engineers I've ever worked with: Joe Venneri and Bobby Bloom.

Bobby went on to record a couple of great songs, including 'Montego Bay.' Sadly, we lost him at an early age. Joey Venneri was a bass player and traveled with The Tokens, and between dates worked with me at Mira setting up the sessions. He was tireless, and it was his motorcycle that was forever captured on 'Leader Of The Pack.' Mira also had a room in the back with a lathe where this outstanding engineer named Alfie cut great ref discs and masters – what an expert! He and I packed a lot of level onto those discs without the stylus skipping.

The girl-group records are particularly well-suited for AM radio. Were you using anything special for playbacks?
Like most of the studios at that time, Mira had the Altec 604 playback monitors, but the difference there was that our 604s were actually *behind* you in the control room. We had a switch at Mira that enabled you to go from mono to stereo and even to a three-track mix – it was like pre-surround sound – it gave you a rush to hear music being played back that way.

For mixing, a lot of engineers were using KLHs and other bookshelf speakers. It was the advent of the near-field monitor age. I came up with my own homemade monitor for mixing mono records, utilizing a plastic Crossley radio with a little speaker inside of it. My formula was to take off the back of the radio, remove all the tubes and guts, keep the speaker in tact, and stuff the rest of that baby with foam rubber. Then I proceeded to seal it up with adhesive tape, and outfit it with a quarter-inch jack. There it was. I'd bet the store that if it sounded good through *that* speaker, it would sound great on the radio.

Looking back, was it luck, skill, or a combination of both that enabled you to make these memorable recordings?
If not for the songs and production vision of people like Jeff Barry, Ellie Greenwich, Carole

King, Gerry Goffin, Lieber & Stoller, George Goldner, Shadow Morton, and Luther Dixon, The Tokens, Mann & Weil, the boys from FGG Productions, and Madera & White, to mention a few, I wouldn't have been part of the whole Red Bird and girl-group era. Had it not been for Jerry Ragovoy, Quincy Jones, and Jerry, Mike, and Luther once again, I would have never developed my R&B chops.

Through my work with of all these artists, I interpreted and merged their sounds and thoughts at the console and felt like I was a player adding a performance. Had there not been a Bert Berns in my corner a little later on, I wouldn't have been on the Van Morrison or Neil Diamond sessions. There's always been someone important every step of the way, providing me with a great opportunity. I know I couldn't have done it without them.

pop takes off

…and Simon, Columbia A at 799 7th Ave., 1967.

By the mid-1960s, the convergence of artists from overlapping generations had turned the charts into a musical battlefield. Louis Armstrong halted the Beatles' hit parade with 'Hello Dolly,' the Lovin' Spoonful deposed Sinatra, Ray Conniff slugged it out with the Yardbirds, the Byrds flew past Dean Martin. It was an unprecedented phenomenon and, in all likelihood, it will never again be repeated.

"I saw the tail-end of the overlapping," says Artie Butler. "I was there when the writers were in these booths and you'd find out that Connie Francis, or Ben E. King, or Sinatra, was coming in for a date and needed a song. Had I been 10 years younger, I couldn't have appreciated that. For that matter, had I been 10 years older, I wouldn't have understood the rock movement when it arrived."

At 30th Street Studios, bastion of the old guard, the incipient rock movement was viewed with suspicion – if not outright disdain. "Mitch Miller wouldn't allow it," says Frank Laico bluntly. "The thing is, Columbia had all this great talent that Mitch had literally discovered, people who no one knew existed previously. Until finally it became obvious that this [rock] was something we had to reckon with. So they decided to just set up a separate operation – which turned out to be Epic. So someone else maintained that division, while Mitch stayed with Columbia."

The increased use of close miking – a hallmark of 1960s rock recordings – was anathema to Laico, a longtime lover of leakage. "I'd close-mic things when people would want it like that, even if it wasn't my first choice," recalls Laico. "It was a sound, you know? It wasn't exactly the way I liked to record. The thing is, bands would come in during that time and they'd want everything to sound like that. Of course, we were in this massive studio using classical microphones, but I would be willing to try it, if that's what it took to make them happy. But even when I'd be doing a rock session like that, I'd still use the best mics we had, even as the trend toward dynamic mics came in."

Many labels begrudgingly signed up rock acts as a way to stay profitable, but in 1965 Columbia could afford to keep its distance. As the company responsible for the introduction of the 33⅓ rpm long-playing record back in 1947, Columbia had managed to dictate the type of music marketed in LP form in the years that followed. In 1948, Columbia's original cast recording of Rodgers and Hammerstein's *South Pacific* became the first successful LP release in history, selling over a million copies and giving Columbia a virtual lock on cast recordings over the next 25 years. *Kismet, Bells Are Ringing, My Fair Lady* and *West Side Story* were just a few of the hit Broadway and movie soundtrack collections issued through the period, many of which were recorded under the supervision of engineer Laico.

Through 1965, Broadway cast, original soundtrack, jazz and light pop continued to drive LP sales. At the same time, the pop crusade launched by the Beatles a year earlier was gathering steam. In the 15 years since Mitch Miller assumed his A&R post, Columbia's pop division had delivered a seemingly endless stream of revenue. Most of it, however, was coming on the strength of artists who were no longer a major threat in the all-important singles market.

Despite their enormous power, major labels like Columbia and RCA still had only marginal rock representation. Bob Dylan, Columbia's folk-era recruit, hadn't yet achieved legendary status; RCA's Elvis Presley, the one-time savior of rock'n'roll, had been reduced to a parody of his former self at the hands of manager Colonel Tom Parker.

With secondary labels continuing to dominate the youth market, it was time for the majors to play catch-up. At Columbia, the effort was spearheaded by a group of up-and-coming producers and engineers, whose studio methods, though markedly different from those of their predecessors, were no less inventive.

LIKE A ROLLING STONE

On December 6th, 1962, Bob Dylan, a 21-year-old Minnesotan-turned-Manhattanite, took the uptown train to Columbia's 799 7th Avenue studio, put a capo on his Martin acoustic and delivered 'A Hard Rain's A-Gonna Fall,' penned four weeks earlier during the U.S-Soviet military stand-off that nearly plunged the world into thermonuclear war.

Though his vision of apocalypse never materialized, 'A Hard Rain's A-Gonna Fall,' 'Masters of War', and Peter, Paul & Mary's cover of 'Blowin' in the Wind' – at the time the fastest-selling single in Columbia Records' history – made Dylan the darling of the political left as 1963 drew to a close.

But with the emergence of the Beatles, Dylan turned away from topical songwriting; within a year, the one-time prince of protest had become master of the three-minute pop song. 'Mr. Tambourine Man,' 'It Ain't Me, Babe,' and 'All I Really Want to Do' all made the Top 10 when covered by The Byrds, The Turtles, and Cher, respectively. Overnight, 'folk rock,' a distillation of acoustic folk and electric pop, ushered in a new direction for Top 40 radio.

Dylan's most important song of the period was a scathing attack on America's well-educated and privileged class (whose members, ironically, comprised a large portion of Dylan's former folk following). With a running time of 6:07, 'Like a Rolling Stone,' which peaked at Number Three in August, proved that a pop smash needn't be resolved in three minutes or less. For the recording on June 16th, CBS producer Tom Wilson joined Dylan and a crew of session players at Columbia's 799 7th Avenue facility, located directly across from Broadway's music-publishing mecca on the corner of West 50th Street. As its name suggests, Studio A – situated seven flights up – was the first studio in the Columbia Records system, operational since the 1930s. Like the 30th Street facility, 799 7th was a decent-sized room, although not nearly as spacious as its crosstown peer.

"On balance, Studio A was a pretty nice place," remembers Frank Laico. "The first Barbra Streisand album was done there; we'd have a 36-piece orchestra for dates like that, and they'd fit just fine. But before we had 30th Street, if there was a really big group coming in, we'd have to go across the street to the playhouse and then send the feed back over to 799.

"Like 30th Street, Studio A had a Fairchild limiter that looked like a huge black box, which I used quite a bit on vocals," says Laico. "Of course we also had limiters right in the console, but that Fairchild was always my favorite. The consoles were all Columbia-built. The recorders were the usual – Ampex 200, 300 mono, two- and three-track early on, four- and eight-track later in the 1960s. They were always being moved from one studio to the next, so there was never any one recorder that remained on the premises.

"Compared to 30th Street, the room was pretty dull-sounding," says Laico, "you really had to work to get the sound right. We were always after R&D to liven it up a bit. They tried but never really succeeded in giving it the kind of presence I wanted, at least compared to what we had over at 30th. For echo, we'd turned the stairwell into a live chamber, with a mic right outside the seventh-floor landing, and an Altec loudspeaker way down below. That set-up worked nicely: it provided some nice natural delay with the echo. Whenever possible, we'd have to ask the superintendent to lock the doors to the stairwell so people wouldn't come barging in!"

Laico, who engineered Dylan's follow-up hit 'Positively 4th Street' and other tracks on Dylan's sixth Columbia effort *Highway 61 Revisited*, remembers that "a Dylan session was completely different – you weren't working with a large band. There was a producer, Tom Wilson, who had things pre-determined. I would talk to the musicians themselves and see how they'd want things set up. Dylan wanted everyone close together – in fact, he wanted to be on top of the drums, which was unique! That was OK – in fact, I never liked it in later years when the bands would be spread apart, to the point that the different players were situated in separate rooms. What's the point?

"I didn't even like using headphones. Unless someone specified, I'd always just roll a big speaker right up there, and then just control the amount of volume. They weren't hearing themselves through the speaker, just the band. I think you can hear the difference."

For the taping of 'Like a Rolling Stone,' Dylan's assembled multitude included ace blues-rock guitarist Mike Bloomfield, drummer Bobby Gregg, pianist Paul Griffin, and, on organ, Al Kooper, a frequent studio hand and co-writer of 'This Diamond Ring,' a Number One hit for Gary Lewis and The Playboys several months earlier. The band had attempted five takes of the song on the previous day, but on the 16th the magic Dylan had been waiting for finally occurred when Kooper settled in behind the organ and let loose with a series of off-the-cuff riffs and embellishments that would become an essential part of Dylan's new sound.

> "FOR ECHO, WE'D TURN THE STAIRWELL INTO A CHAMBER, WITH A MIC ON THE 7TH-FLOOR LANDING AND A SPEAKER WAY DOWN BELOW."

In reality, Kooper knew very little about organ playing; he simply wanted in on the session. "I'm fortunate that I was able to pull it off like that," muses Kooper. "You have to have complete self-confidence to walk out there like that and make it work. I was walking a thin line, working with an unfamiliar instrument – but I just heard it and went for it, and Tom Wilson made sure it went down the right way."

As it turns out, Kooper wasn't the only one fumbling his way to greatness that afternoon. 'Like a Rolling Stone' became the first rock session for soon-to-be engineering great Roy Halee, who'd spent the previous six years editing classical works over at the label's East 52nd Street location. "Columbia, at the time, had this reputation of being a pop record company," recalls Halee. "They definitely frowned on rock'n'roll. Everybody's attitude was, 'Who needs this? We've got Percy Faith and Ray Conniff!' As soon as I got into the studio, Dylan came in, and all of a sudden, I was the reigning king of rock'n'roll! Which was funny – because, quite honestly, I had no idea what I was doing. But the music catered to experimentation, which was perfect for someone like me. I really was at the right place at the right time, because from that day forward, I ended up doing most of the label's contemporary stuff."

With 'Like a Rolling Stone,' Columbia finally had a bona fide 'hip' hit record on the charts. That fall, Tom Wilson was encouraged to go and find a few more just like it. When nothing suitable turned up right away, he went into the vault and patched one together from scratch.

THE SOUNDS OF SIMON

In late 1963, Paul Simon, an ambitious young song plugger with Marks Music, convinced Tom Wilson that his backlog of brooding, urban folk songs was worthy of a

Columbia recording contract. By the time Simon and childhood pal Art Garfunkel convened inside Columbia's 799 7th Avenue studios the following March, the world was a different place. One month earlier the Beatles had landed, irrevocably changing the musical landscape. Though expertly crafted and brimming with the meticulous harmony lines that would later make Simon & Garfunkel stars, their debut album *Wednesday Morning 3 AM* hit the streets with a resounding thud. A frustrated Simon packed his bags and headed for England, leaving Garfunkel to resume his studies at Columbia University. End of story.

Not quite. Fast-forward to the fall of 1965. Folk-rock has taken the country by storm, on the strength of hits like the Byrds' 'Mr. Tambourine Man' and Bob Dylan's 'Like a Rolling Stone.' Out of nowhere, record companies were raking in the dough with songs of social and political import. If it had a backbeat, it had a shot at the top.

In New York, Tom Wilson noticed that one of the tracks from *Wednesday Morning 3 AM*, entitled 'The Sound of Silence,' had been attracting listener attention at stations along the East Coast. On a whim, Wilson decided to capitalize on the interest by fortifying the track with a rock combo. There was only one small problem: though still contracted to Columbia, for the time being Simon & Garfunkel were no longer a working entity.

That didn't deter Wilson, who rang up four of New York's most trusted session hands – bassist Joe Mack, guitarists Al Gorgoni and Vinnie Bell, and drummer Buddy Salzman – and with help from engineer Roy Halee began the task of breathing new life into Simon's acoustic classic, unknown to Simon himself.

By 1966, Al Gorgoni had worked hundreds of sessions in studios all over the New York, helping to pump out hits for The Coasters, The Four Seasons, The Shangri-Las and many others. "'The Sound of Silence' just knocked me out the first time I heard it," recalls Gorgoni. "At the time I was working across the street at April Blackwood with [songwriter] Chip Taylor. After the session I told Chip about this tune I'd just worked, how amazing it sounded. I mean, the song was already great in its original form – it just needed that extra touch to put it over the top and turn it into a hit."

Transforming 'The Sound of Silence' was no easy task. For starters, the tempo on the original 1964 backing track (which consisted of two acoustic guitars and upright bass) was uneven, making overdubbing difficult. Nor did Wilson wish to bury S&G's compelling vocal sound under a hail of twangy guitars.

"We were all just trying really hard to get it together and stay with the recording, though I think I'm a little on top of it in spots," says Gorgoni. "I remember listening to Paul's acoustic guitar part through the headphones and basically just copping it. I had this Epiphone Casino, which had the right sound. People used to think it was a 12-string electric like the Byrds – it's not, it's just me and Vinnie playing together mixed together onto the same track. And Vinnie added a few bluesy fills that you can hear in there as well. It took us a couple hours and it was done."

In an obvious homage to the Byrds' successful formula, Halee juiced the entire rhythm track with a touch of slap-back echo. "That's a record-business concept – if it worked once, do it again," says Gorgoni. "But it's a really cool sound – Roy made it fit beautifully."

Released on November 25th, 'The Sound of Silence' immediately began rising up the Hot 100. Incredibly, Columbia still hadn't alerted its author, who discovered he had a hit on his hands only after picking up a copy of *Billboard* in a London bookstore. Back in America, a reformed Simon & Garfunkel quickly prepared a batch of songs written by Simon during his UK residency, this time with the help of a rock rhythm section. The duo responded to the pressure of instant and unexpected stardom by cutting what would become their next two singles – 'Homeward Bound' and 'I Am a Rock' – in a single afternoon.

Time hasn't changed Al Gorgoni's opinion of the technical patchwork that made 'The Sound of Silence' a number one hit and Simon and Garfunkel a household name. "I hate it," laughs Gorgoni. "I mean, I love the song – but those guitars … they're just awful. I really can't listen to it now. I took it out for this occasion just to hear it again – but that was enough. Of course, all the things that are wrong with the recording didn't stop it from becoming a huge success. So there you go."

the summer of
the spoonful

n the summer of 1966, a year that would go down as the most significant 12 months in the history of rock, New York's leading musical trendsetters were also its most commercially successful outfit. The Lovin' Spoonful had scored four consecutive Top 10 hits with 'Do You Believe in Magic,' 'You Didn't Have to Be So Nice,' 'Did You Ever Have To Make Up Your Mind,' and 'Daydream.'

Blending pop-song melodies with a Greenwich Village folk sensibility, writer John Sebastian had single-handedly kept The Spoonful on the chart over the previous nine months; his granny glasses and autoharp gave the band a striking visual image as well. In Joe Butler, The Spoonful had an unswerving rhythm man; while bassist Steve Boone offered solid songwriting relief.

And yet it might all have been completely different had it not been for The Spoonful's brilliant, zany lead guitarist, Toronto-born Zal Yanovsky, who'd met Sebastian while watching the Beatles make their debut on the Ed Sullivan Show two years earlier. In a business populated by rote accompanists, Yanovsky was an original, a charismatic live wire whose good taste and youthful versatility gave the Spoonful endless appeal. An unfortunate marijuana bust that spring would make *Hums Of The Lovin' Spoonful* his swan song. But that LP, the band's fourth in the space of a year, would become its finest collection of all.

Much has been made of the countrified efforts of groups like the Byrds, Buffalo Springfield, and the Flying Burrito Brothers. Yet it was the Spoonful who laid it down first with *Hums*, an Erik Jacobsen-produced album packed with traditional folk- and country-based originals and using authentic instrumentation such as dobro, pedal steel guitar, bass marimba, and open-tuned 12-string.

It was Yanovsky's reverb-laden country bends and arpeggios – performed on his favorite axe, an early 1960s Guild Thunderbird – that gave Sebastian's 'Darlin' Companion,' 'Lovin' You,' and especially 'Nashville Cats' the depth they deserved. "I'd bought that guitar new at Manny's around 1964," says Yanovsky. "Right after 'Do You Believe in Magic' I'd replaced the original Guild pickups with humbuckers, which weren't quite as warm as the originals, but they aged nicely."

Yanovsky's true talent, however, was his ability to craft guitar parts that clashed with – rather than complemented – the underlying track. For 'Rain on the Roof,' Yanovsky accented the dream-like 6- and 12-string acoustics (performed by Yanovsky and Sebastian together) with a few jolting blasts from his Thunderbird. "I used to record mainly with a Super Reverb, which is what I used on that record," says Yanovsky. "A lot of bottom and very loud, which you can really hear on 'Rain on the Roof.' And I almost always went straight in, though I'd occasionally use this thing called a Treble Booster, which helped with those horrible Standel amps we used to use on stage." Like most groundbreaking acts of the mid 1960s, the Spoonful were eager to expand their sonic boundaries once inside the studio. "During that time we were recording at places like Bell Sound and Allegro," says Yanovsky. "The first album was done on four-track, which was great; we just went in and nailed it. Then we began working with Roy Halee at Columbia's Studio A."

The technical explorations that would quickly become Halee's trademark began that summer at 799 7th Avenue. Halee's chief weapon was his use of echo – the homemade variety. "I loved ambience – I needed to hear that as part of the overall sound," says Halee, who provided the opening 'kick' heard on *Hum* masterpiece 'Summer in the City' by miking up an empty garbage can; he then ran the entire track out into the studio's stairwell echo-chamber. "I've always loved studios that had a warmth to them, and the rooms where I recorded with the Spoonful were large. They could hold a number of musicians, but they were workable in that they could be deadened if need be, or opened up to get as much ambience as you want. But I'd always go for leakage – it just made everything sound fuller and more alive."

With an unbroken string of hit singles behind them, no one would have blamed the Spoonful for playing it safe on *Hums*. Instead, the band crafted an album that took chances, paid homage to old heroes – and yet still managed to rack up an additional four hit singles, including the three-week chart-topper 'Summer in the City.'

That fall, the Spoonful were set to track a new collection of songs for inclusion in the Francis Ford Coppola film *You're a Big Boy Now*. This was their second such project: earlier that year, Woody Allen had featured the group in his oddball comedy *What's Up, Tiger Lily?* This time, the location was Phil Ramone's A&R Studio, two blocks down from Columbia. At the controls was Brooks Arthur, who'd recently accepted an offer to join the A&R team.

"Phil found me at Mira Sound," recalls Arthur, "and asked me to come over to A&R to work in a partnership. I went down and met Don Frye and all the rest of the guys at Phil's place, and so decided to take him up on it. Phil took out this full-page ad in the trade papers that read, 'Brooks Arthur has a new home: A&R.' I'll never forget that."

Nor would Arthur forget the session that produced John Sebastian's 'Darling Be Home Soon,' slated to be The Spoonful's next single. "On 'Darling' we were recording to four-track," recalls Arthur, "and we'd finished the basic track and were getting set to add the strings and horns. Now all we had was one open track, so it came down to wiping John's guide vocal in order to have track two and track four available for each section. So I turned to the producer, affectionately known around town as 'Crazy Jack,' and asked if that would be OK, and he said, 'Yep.' So I set it up, but, just to be on the safe side, right before I hit 'record' I asked Jack one more time, 'You sure?'

"Once again, he says yes, so I go ahead and do the take. When it was finished we spooled it back for a listen. At A&R they had four speakers set up to be dedicated, one for each track, so you could actually hear the parts individually through each speaker. We were just rolling the tape when Jack looks over and says, 'Let me hear John's vocal.' I'm not kidding!

"My heart went into my stomach. I started to say, 'Um, Jack, you told me to …' and right at that instant he starts punching me, I'm up against the wall, I start punching right back, the whole room's going nuts, Zal is watching all this from the studio totally freaked out. Finally, Phil rushes over and gets between us to break it up. Just as Jack's leaving, Sebastian suddenly walks in, looks down at the blinking record lights on the tape machine, realizes what's happened, and blurts out, 'Good thing! I hated that vocal anyway!'"

RESCUING ARETHA

She'd been recording professionally since the age of 12, including six years with a major label, and yet most people had never heard of 25-year-old Aretha Franklin when 'I Never Loved a Man (The Way I Love You),' her debut single for Atlantic Records, hit the charts in March 1967. Columbia, which had signed Franklin in 1960, had attempted to mold the skilled gospel singer and pianist into a Dinah Washington-styled pop balladeer. The result was one minor hit by 1966. Long before her CBS contract expired, a frustrated Franklin had even contemplated retirement.

Enter Jerry Wexler, president of Atlantic Records. In Franklin, Wexler saw the makings of a world-class artist who'd simply been working for the wrong team. Realizing that the label's soul and R&B lineage was far closer to the spirit of her gospel roots,

■ **ARTIE BUTLER (producer-arranger) "The thing about Atlantic during the 1960s was that sound – it wasn't a huge studio, only around 20 by 40 feet or so. And there was practically no separation in there as well. You can hear it – and that was the magic of those records! It was a really live kind of 'round' sound. They had a vocal booth, but there wasn't any drum booth or anything like that – in fact, they had the drums out in the middle of the room, which is why the drums are all over those records. Just a beautiful sound."**

Franklin signed on with Wexler's group in late 1966 and prepared for a one-week session to record a new album.

In mid-January, 1967, Wexler took Franklin down to the small town of Muscle Shoals, Alabama, to try to achieve the right atmosphere. With them went Ted White, her husband and manager. Muscle Shoals was the home of Rick Hall's Fame Recording Studios. For the previous two years, Wexler had used Fame Studios, Stax Studios in Memphis, and other ramshackle facilities in the Muscle Shoals region to put together the bulk of Atlantic's soul output.

"The thing about the Southern style of recording was that the players didn't work from completed arrangements on paper. The records were all built spontaneously off chord charts, with each chord being numbered," says Wexler. "They'd just have the song laid out in front of them, and what they excelled at was coming up with the 'in-betweens' – the pick-up notes, the turnarounds, the walk-downs, the walk-ups – on the spot. Once somebody came up with a one- or two-bar pattern, they were off."

After years of struggling within Columbia's controlled recording environment, Wexler knew that the looseness of Fame's house section – which included guitarist Jimmy Johnson, pianist Spooner Oldham and drummer Roger Hawkins – was just what Franklin needed. "That's what made those players so great," says Wexler. "It was obvious they'd be a good fit for Aretha."

And yet no one could have guessed just *how* good it would all sound until Aretha walked through the door, sat down at the piano and proceeded to hammer out the framework for 'I Never Loved a Man (The Way I Love You),' written by her songwriting chum Ronnie Shannon.

Having worked with Wilson Pickett on 'Mustang Sallly' and Percy Sledge on 'When a Man Loves a Woman,' the Fame crew was used to powerhouse talent – but this was something different. In no time, an inspired Oldham concocted a rhythmic Wurlitzer piano intro, the band fell into the groove, Franklin sang live – and within a few hours, 'I Never Loved a Man' was in the bag. "We couldn't believe what we were hearing during that playback," says Wexler. "It was just incredible."

But the high emotions quickly turned heated when Ted White and a member of Fame's white horn section began exchanging racial remarks. Within hours a full-blown, alcohol-assisted altercation between White and Rick Hall ended any hopes of further Southern session work.

"There was no way Aretha was going to be comfortable returning to that studio," says Wexler, who nevertheless wasn't about to give up on the magical formula that had produced Franklin's first offering. "I knew she was very comfortable with the musicians, however. So it was essential that we get them back together for the rest of the album."

And quickly. No sooner had Wexler leaked acetates of 'I Never Loved a Man' to a few prominent DJs than request lines began lighting up across the country. Franklin's six-year drought had come to a screeching halt – but all Wexler had to offer was one song. Wexler immediately put in a call to Johnson, Oldham and Hawkins, described the situation, then told them to hop on the next flight to Kennedy (in the process conveniently forgetting to tell their boss, Rick Hall). Days later, the crew, looking very much like three hayseeds in the big city, arrived at Atlantic's 60th Street studio, ready to roll.

"With Aretha," says Wexler, "we would very carefully and meticulously record the rhythm section live, perhaps with the horns, or sometimes with the horns added later. Aretha would be playing the piano and singing simultaneously, which immediately brought in the monumental problem of leakage – voice into piano, or conversely.

"Not that we wanted to discourage her from working that way – she was a fantastic player, and being at the piano really brought out the Aretha-ness in Aretha. So what we'd do is rehearse it and rehearse it, and when we got what we thought was the penultimate take – and I emphasize penultimate – we made one more take where she didn't sing. And then she'd super-impose a lead vocal over that take. And almost invariably that would be the take that went out.

"So many times during the making of that record, as well as the others that followed, I'd be in the control room with Tom Dowd as the recording was going down, and we'd be thinking, 'Oh my God, this is awesome.' And at the end of the take I'd yell out, 'That's it, that was the take!' And she'd call back, 'No, not yet.' Because in her mind, she'd already be thinking of some unbelievable vocal inversions that we couldn't possibly have dreamed of that she was going to do on the very next take!"

In a matter of weeks, Franklin's debut album for Atlantic, *I Never Loved a Man (The Way I Love You)*, was complete. Along with the hit title track (which rode into the Top Ten that April), *I Never Loved a Man* included Franklin's soulful rendering of 'Do Right Woman, Do Right Man,' written by Fame staffers Chips Moman and Dan Penn the day of the Muscle Shoals session and part-recorded there. But it was the album's opener, a stunning cover of Otis Redding's 'Respect' (featuring vocal back-ups by Franklin's sisters Carolyn and Erma), that gave Franklin her first Number One single – and brought her the richly deserved title of 'Queen of Soul.'

The album that broke Franklin to the world would also affect the lives of all involved. Earlier tensions between Franklin and her volatile husband came to a boil over the Muscle Shoals incident; within months, their marriage was permanently on the rocks.

Miffed by Wexler's clandestine hiring of his golden rhythm section, Hall quickly ended all business affairs with Atlantic; his feud with Wexler would last for decades. In turn, Johnson, Hawkins and company, having tasted life on the outside, would go on to form their own enterprise, Muscle Shoals Sound Studios, just up the road from Hall's Fame facility. They would give their former boss a run for his money in the years to come.

INTERVIEW JERRY WEXLER and ARIF MARDIN

Perhaps more than any other label owner in history, Atlantic's Jerry Wexler understood his artists. Wexler frequently turned one-shot wonders at competing labels into hit-making icons at Atlantic. Under the guidance of Wexler and Ahmet Ertegun, Ray Charles went from floundering Nat Cole wannabe to "legendary genius of soul" – in the space of four years. During the 1960s, Wexler tamed temperamental talents like Solomon Burke and Wilson Pickett. With Wexler's guidance, Aretha Franklin redefined soul music and became, in all probability, the most significant artist in Atlantic's 50-year-history. His secret? Not forcing his talent to do anything that didn't fit the bill. "I urged Aretha to just be Aretha," Wexler once said. "I just helped her find her true voice."

Few producers left on the planet are as accomplished both technically and musically as Turkish-born Arif Mardin, who arrived in the US in the late 1950s, took a degree at Boston's Berklee College of Music, and talked his way into Atlantic's bustling independent empire a short time later. Handed the job of house arranger, Mardin quickly brought an air of sophistication to Atlantic's rootsy R&B sound. Today, the swirling woodwinds and strings that color 'Until You Come Back to Me' and other great Aretha Franklin recordings are testament to Mardin's enormous musicality. Mardin's production work with the likes of Average White Band, and, in particular, the Bee Gees, helped spark the disco inferno of the mid-1970s. In addition to Franklin, Mardin's leading ladies include Chaka Khan, Roberta Flack, Jewel, and, most recently, Norah Jones, for whom Mardin produced and arranged the multiple Grammy-winning *Come Away With Me*.

Back in those days, how involved were you in the control-room, button-pushing aspect of the recording process?

JERRY WEXLER I didn't always pay attention to the technical stuff, that was the engineer's business. I was concerned with the musical aspect of the business. The way I see it, a producer is someone who can change the music only when needed. Whether it's the bass line, or the tempo, if you have to change the chords in the bridge, or shorten eight-bar bridges to four-bar bridges. That's why it's so important to be able to work on the music only when it's needed – that time when you reach the point when something needs to be done because suddenly you've hit the wall and you're in a box. What does the producer do? I've seen a lot of these guys say, "Well, give me another one." And they just move on. George Martin did that – he led the Beatles out of the desert and into the land of milk and honey.

Could you paint a picture of the inside of Atlantic's West 60th Street studio during the 1960s and 1970s?

ARIF MARDIN 60th Street was a cutting-edge facility at the time, and a really good-sized place as well. We could have 20 strings, three guitars, bass, drums, organ, piano, and a vocal group. And we could get them far enough separated that we could still have a great live session. Tom Dowd, visionary engineer that he was – and still is – made all the decisions about reverb, EQ, level, right there as the recording was going down.

What were those mixing sessions like?

WEXLER Loud. [laughs] They always talk about Brian Wilson being deaf in one ear. Well Bob Crewe's deaf in one ear, Jerry Leiber's deaf in one ear, and Tommy Dowd's hearing in one ear was questionable as well. You know why? Because they were always listening way too loud all of those years. When I'd be in the studio with Jerry Leiber during a playback or something, I would have to stand between him and the volume control – I wouldn't let him get near it. Because he would always run the fucker up. It would drive me crazy. Under the guise that "loud music is good music." Now if I had a mythical servant, who could go to every home, juke box, radio station, wherever my music is playing, and make my song louder than all the rest, I've got the world by the balls. But in my opinion, it's not always in the best interest of the music.

MARDIN Mixing was a lot of fun at that time, because so much of the sound was determined during the recording process with microphone placement, and so on. There was less you could do to change things in the mix other than relationships between parts, and EQ. Things like that. It was truly an art form.

Is there some aspect of your studio routine that hasn't changed?

The idea of capturing a performance – that's always there. And of course what makes a great performance possible is a great song. In that respect, it doesn't really matter if you're recording on a 1950s mono Ampex or using unlimited tracks and totally digitized. Getting what you hear in the room onto the recorder, that's the important part. If there's a little effect that I like, I'll put it on tape right there. I've always preferred to make those decisions as I'm going along. Because if I don't, I'll have to make that decision later on. This way, it saves a lot of time ... and money.

Many of your best records were built on the premise that tracks should be cut live.
It's always much better to work with the musicians you have on hand in the room. Those Aretha sessions with Cornell Dupree, Donny Hathaway, Bernard Purdie, Chuck Rainey ... it all went down right there, totally live. Tracks aren't everything. A little while ago I was working on a dance re-mix of Aretha's 'Rock Steady' with my son Joe, who is a producer and engineer.

And when I pulled up the track sheet, it was amazing. It said things like, "Drums – stereo." That was it! You know, stereo drums! Tom Dowd thought that was a luxury! Now we have eight tracks for drums. But when you listen to that song, that Bernard Purdie sound is captured right there on a really basic stereo drum track. It's not always the number of tracks, it's being able to use your ears that counts the most. And yet even with all the technical capability, a lot of younger engineers still don't know how to mic a drum set properly.

WEXLER Even though our main objective in the studio was capturing a live performance, we understood early on the advantages of having the technology at your disposal. Later on, a lot of critics would inform us about a particular record and say things like, "Well, you know, that had to have been a live vocal, it's so warm!" And my response to that would be, "You can't possibly know that."

You see the whole thing about recording is the attempt at verisimilitude – not truth, but the appearance of truth. And that's what we would set out to achieve. And you get there not with tricks and schtick, but with music – it's the key to all of this. If you get the music right both in rehearsal and recording, you could just sit there and never touch a single fader.

It's often struck me that Atlantic Records' idea of the way in which American black music should sound was considerably different from the vision that Berry Gordy had over at Motown.
I was a great admirer of Berry – he figured out how to make music that was created and performed by black composers and players instantly palatable to white teenagers. He didn't even have to go the route of having it happen on R&B stations first. It's one of the most brilliant successes in the history of the music business. They had those little romance vignettes, with James Jamerson laying down the bass bottom, and everyone bought it and loved it. Motown became the standard rubric for black music.

To the point that, to this day, people still think of your music as "Motown music."
Which is a great tribute to Berry. That's why nowadays it takes people with more of an acute consciousness to distinguish between Motown and all of our music: early Atlantic, southern Atlantic, Memphis, Muscle Shoals, Miami. Which was closer to the root.

Which is fine for the Smithsonian or the critics, but it didn't get us the fantastic global recognition that Motown got. People hear Wilson Pickett today and they think, "Motown." It becomes the rubric for generations of people. It's the best measure of how much Berry Gordy accomplished. It takes people who are true fans – not just listeners – to have the energy and the drive to make that distinction.

How does one distinguish a Motown record from an Atlantic soul record? Is it the bottom? Al Jackson's kick drum locking with the bass – things like that?
When we first started out, people used to talk about the "Atlantic sound," which Tommy Dowd helped us achieve. Which was kind of a clean funk. Our records were in tune and in time. Go back and listen to some of the doo-wop records that preceded ours. You could throw up.

Chips Moman once said, "It's all in the upbeats." The unexpected, syncopated upbeat, the notes you leave out, the pick-up notes … and suddenly you have a rhythm pattern. And that's what they did so well. I backed off on the two and four. Motown was more of a walking four; Bob Crewe had done the same thing with the 4 Seasons. Bob would walk that beat on a piece of wood that would be miked. But I didn't always like that – this procession of inexorable downbeats.

Atlantic's 60th Street studio had a very identifiable sound …
It wasn't just the physical aspects of that room per se, but the players who worked that room – they gave the room its character. That's the sound you hear on those records.

What techniques might you use in the studio in order to make the artist feel more comfortable?
If they played an instrument, even with indifferent players I'd put them in the mix, just to have them playing. Somehow, it would always act like a roadmap for the singer, to bring out his or her essence.

Is that why you often see Aretha seated at the piano in those studio photos?
Yes, but with Aretha, because she was such a great singer, it sometimes had the opposite effect. The thing is, when Aretha was freed from the piano and could really put her mind

into it, she would always come up with some really incredible vocal inversions. So we would almost always have her re-cut her vocal as an overdub.

Nowadays even the most basic digital recorder will let you cut and paste parts in no time flat. Of course, the was a time when you really had to work for it.

MARDIN Oh yes. One time, Tom and I were cutting Aretha at Atlantic. She'd just finished recording an amazing vocal – a portion of which we then managed to erase! So we had to go up to her and say, "Look, punish us, but can you please sing that last bridge again?" And she said, "I already did – on the previous track." And she turns to leave the studio and adds, "I'm sure you can figure it out."

And we're looking at each other going, "Previous take? What are we supposed to do with that?" [laughs] I mean, there was no click, it was a totally different tempo. So we sat down and transferred her vocal track to mono, and then phrase by phrase we reconstructed the bridge. Just like sampling—only doing it manually, with tape. But we did it.

Atlantic was initially built on the premise that having a lot of great equipment doesn't necessarily guarantee a lot of great records.

That's why I'm always telling people, save your money! A little while ago I bought a recording of Mussorgsky's *Pictures at an Exhibition*, recorded in 1951 by the Chicago Symphony. And the performance was so warm and clear and wonderful. Then my son looks at the album cover and says, 'Look, Dad – one U47.' That was it! Nevertheless, they made this beautiful-sounding record anyway. So there you go.

the bang
records story

As a leading talent finder for Atlantic Records, producer/A&R man Bert Berns had proved his worth many times over, attracting major players such as The (Young) Rascals, Van Morrison, The McCoys and others since joining in 1961. Berns was also a top-class songwriter who managed to parlay the same I-IV-V chord progression into innumerable pop and R&B classics, from the Isley Brothers' 'Twist and Shout' (later covered to perfection by the Beatles) and the McCoy's 'Hang On Sloopy' to Erma Franklin's 1967 masterpiece 'Piece of My Heart,' later a massive rock hit for Janis Joplin.

In the mid 1960s, Atlantic rewarded Berns for five years of hard work by forming a subsidiary, Bang Records, designed specifically for Berns' production efforts. Its name was based on the initials of Atlantic's main players: B (Bert Berns), A (Ahmet Ertegun), N (Nesuhi Ertegun) and G (Gerald Wexler).

Among Berns's earliest and most successful clients was Brooklyn-born songwriting dynamo Neil Diamond, whose run of acoustic-guitar based hit singles began with a simple demo cut in the spring of 1966 at Dick Charles Studios.

"Jeff Barry, Ellie Greenwich and I were sitting around talking about material for my first session for the label," recalls Diamond. "I began to play a guitar lick which caught Jeff's ear. His positive reaction made me go home and finish 'Cherry Cherry.' We all went into Dick Charles' studio and recorded a pared-down demo version. Jeff and Ellie sang the background parts, I sang and played the guitar, and Artie Butler played the piano and Hammond organ. I forgot who played bass but bless him anyway."

"The bassist was a guy named Dick Romoff, who recently passed away," recalls Artie Butler, Diamond's longtime arranger. "We used upright bass on both of those songs, and I remember thinking there was something very organic about that sound during those two recordings. The Fender bass had become very popular by then, obviously, but the electric hadn't taken over completely – you still had options. Upright had an earthier quality, a roundness, that your electric basses don't have."

"Afterwards we overdubbed some hand claps and a few other rhythm things, though we never used a drum," says Diamond, "and we used that demo as the basis for an 'official' recording with horns, voices and drums. Although the big version had lots of energy, it lacked the simplicity and groove of the demo. So the demo was released as my second single on Bang. It was the big hit and a major commercial kick off to my career. I think we made the right choice."

"After 'Cherry, Cherry,' we moved up to A&R for the next big batch of Neil sessions," says Brooks Arthur, Diamond's engineer throughout the Bang years and beyond. "All that stuff: 'Thank the Lord for the Night Time,' 'Kentucky Woman,' 'You Got to Me.'

Later after I'd opened Century Sound, we went in and finished 'Sweet Caroline' there.

"In the studio, it would be Neil on acoustic guitar, Al Gorgoni also on acoustic, with Hugh McCracken on electric, Herb Lavelle on drums. There was Artie Butler on the piano, Ellie Greenwich, Mikey Harris, or a couple of R&B girls perhaps. The group was always pretty close together, and we were using some gobos, but with all those mics open in the room, you learn to use that leakage to your advantage. Leakage could always do great things for microphones!

"The essence of Neil's vocals was almost always live – he'd just come back and touch them up where needed. But it was all basically live to four-track. We'd double the girls, as I had been doing, sometimes even triple them, which was pretty inventive at the time. And change their places as well.

"At A&R we had two four-tracks, and I used them both. And I used the same mic set up as I had at Mira, Associated and Dick Charles – including that Altec underneath and the 57 on the snare. I'd mic the acoustics using either a Sony C-37 or even a Neumann 87. From that point forward I had a pretty serious complement of microphones. Though it's the same mic scheme, it does sound different, because now we're at A&R!

"It was that room – a beautiful cement floor plus the reverb. Plus the real difference at A&R was the tape delay used on the chamber, which always sounded sensational. In fact, I'd never used a delayed chamber at Mira Sound; it wasn't until I got to A&R that I began working that way, but from then on, it really became part of my sound."

In early 1967, Berns convinced Van Morrison, the former lead singer of Them, based in Belfast, Northern Ireland, to return to New York to cut a solo record. Them had previously scored in 1965 with Berns's three-chord classic 'Here Comes the Night.' Among the Morrison originals included on the Bang collection *Blowin' Your Mind* was an acoustic pop ballad entitled 'Brown Eyed Girl,' recorded live by Brooks Arthur up at A&R Studio, featuring the guitar work of session ace Al Gorgoni, who crafted the song's unique riff and melodic fills on the spot.

"Van played the song on his acoustic guitar so we could hear how it went," recalls Gorgoni. "It had this Calypso kind of feel, so I said, 'Oh cool, well then I could do something like this,' and I just started playing this fingerstyle kind of thing on my Gibson L-5, just sort of mimicking that style. We ran it down a couple of times; by the time they pushed the button, I had a pretty good idea of where it was going.

"It was a nice day, I was feeling pretty loose, it was just one of those things that came out right. I mean, it's not Bach or anything. As a session player, you want to get into a place as often as possible where the music just plays itself, where you're not really thinking about what you're doing. And that was one of those times for me. Usually that was the stuff that came out the best.

"There are actually two versions of the song – one was the single, the other has a completely different guitar part on it, from another take. Of course it all just goes in one ear and out the other for me now."

MASTERS OF TALENT

"I'd answered an advert in the local papers looking for British groups to come to America to make hit records," recalls producer/engineer Chris Huston. "It was from a place called Talentmasters Recording Studio, on 126 West 42nd Street. And they ended up picking my group, The Undertakers, as well as Pete Best's combo, to come to America."

As a native Liverpudlian in the era of Beatles world domination, Huston had every right to believe that an enormously successful music career was awaiting him. As it turns out, he was right – but for different reasons altogether. Months after arriving in the States, The Undertakers splintered. While planning his next move, Huston began doing odds and ends around the Talentmasters facilities.

"Because we were being managed by the Talentmasters guys, we got to hang around the studio quite a bit," says Huston. "There were a lot of black groups coming in, people like Chuck Rainey, Bernard Purdie, Eric Gale. We got to see firsthand the way these records were being made, and it was incredibly exciting. It was so completely different from when we were recording for Pye in England – they used to have engineers walking around in white lab coats, who'd set the tone and volume on our amps and in no time proceed to take the balls right out of our music. But not here – everything had so much energy, it was hard to believe.

"At that point, I didn't want to play any more – I just wanted to be on the other side of the glass," says Huston. "So that's when I started. At that time, I was really one of the few engineers with a music background – most just didn't have a music background, simply because at that point it was more of an electronics job than a musical job."

Talentmasters co-owner Bob Gallo picked up on Huston's youthful enthusiasm and decided to give him a shot in the business. "He was an incredible guy," says Huston, "Bob saw something in me that I didn't see in myself at the time. He was the one who got me going – without his constant guidance and goading, I never could have made it.

"The Young Rascals had been signed by Atlantic, and they were just incredible – amazing singers, Davey and Eddie Brigati, who'd been working as Joey Dee and the Starlighters just a few years earlier. So there they were, recording at Talentmasters. I'd only been on the scene for just a short while, but in no time I was recording the Rascals, the Vagrants, all these amazing groups."

At the time, Atlantic, a label known for its chronic studio-hopping, began sending artists like Benny King, the Drifters, Solomon Burke, Mary Wells, and Patti LaBelle over to Talentmasters to cut sessions. Says Huston, "I would get these little notes from Jerry Wexler, saying, 'Chris, I'm sending a new group down to you, tell me how we can benefit from re-recording them.' So there I was doing A&R stuff, or engineering the sessions with Bob Gallo. In the end Atlantic just decided to buy out Gallo and partner Bob Harvey, because all of their acts were recording there anyway, they might as well just own the studio. So that's what they did."

Like some of the independents in the Times Square region, Talentmasters had an interior that was anything but easy on the eye. "When I got there, they had a hollow-core door to the studio," says Huston, "and a single pane of glass on the control room. They also had one Altec 604e speaker for playbacks. The 604e had been developed for the movies – it had what they called the 'academy curve,' nothing above 8000 cycles, nothing below 80. So that meant you had to have your nose bleeding at 5000 in order to know you had anything at 10,000."

Talentmasters did have a quartet of Ampex MX10 mixers, three inputs per mixer in a rack, with four Pultecs fastened right before the inputs of the tape machine. "We had a pair of Ampex four-track machines, 350 and 351," says Huston. "But the thing is we were still documenting a performance, as opposed to creating a performance, which has been the norm for years now."

Over the next two years at Talentmasters, Huston figured in innumerable classic tracks for the likes of James Brown, The Rascals, Mitch Ryder, Don Covay and other top talent, each bearing the imprint of Huston's favorite echo device, a Fisher K-10 spring reverb unit. "There were a total of four units, one for each track, strapped to the rear of the console," notes Huston. "If you listen to 'Groovin'' by the Rascals or James Brown's 'It's a Man's, Man's, Man's World,' you're hearing those spring echoes – that's all it was. Each input was basically an MX10 with a Pultec after it, with a Fisher spring reverb. Before I left, I built a live chamber in there, but for the most part, it was the springs.

"When I was doing the James Brown records, I decided that I wanted to delay the chamber," says Huston, "but also do tape echo that was in time with the vocals. So I went down to Harvey Radio and asked the guy how I could slow down an Ampex recorder." He did it by driving the tape machine from an oscillator that allowed him to alter its speed.

Initially, large-group sessions with clients like Brown proved especially challenging for Huston. "I'd be trying to record these big rhythm sections – horns, background singers, extra guitars, another keyboard, and other instruments as well – with 12 microphones feeding into four tracks," says Huston. "So I came up with this idea: I took some clip leads and put them on the backs of the amplifiers, then I built this junction box and I put the clip leads on it leading from the amplifiers, and it worked perfectly!

"It was a sub-mixer, but it was coming directly from the speakers! But it allowed me to combine all the different signals – which was fine, because the whole rhythm track was going into just one recording track anyway. I built a bunch of them for Mira Sound, several for Atlantic as well. We'd just fasten the things right to the baffles! I mean, it was pretty archaic – you had to make sure the polarity was set properly, or else you'd get this tremendous shock – but it really did the job.

"Back in those days, your job was to walk around the studio and see where the energy was, and get that energy on tape," says Huston. "That might mean bringing out parts of the arrangement that weren't necessarily intended to be a focal point. Or while you're walking the floor during a take you might notice two members of the rhythm section really playing off each other, and you'd run back into the control room and push those two guys up into the mix, 'cause you know intuitively that something's happening there.

"That's what happened on 'Cool Jerk' by The Capitols: I distinctly remember pushing the bass up in response to what I was hearing during the work-up of that song. And that really propelled the take, because if the bass wasn't as prominent, it would have been a completely different song."

For Huston, being in the heart of Manhattan during the most effervescent period in pop music never got lost its appeal. "I used to sleep on the couch at Talentmasters, and on those nights I'd wander around Times Square, which was just a stone's throw from the studio," says Huston. "I'd often wind up in these great clubs they had along Broadway. One night I heard a band that was called The Pigeons, and they were great.

"Afterwards I took them back to the studio, we grabbed some Sicilian pizza downstairs beforehand, then went upstairs, set up and did some demos, which I later took over to Atlantic. They wound up signing these guys right away, but first changed the name of the band to Vanilla Fudge. But this was the way it was back then – I'd literally be doing sessions from eight in the morning until seven at night, go out, hit the clubs, stay up until all hours, then get right back at it again first thing the next morning."

THE WHO BREAK THROUGH

Huston was sitting pretty when Atlantic's braintrust handed the keys to Bert Burns as part of the Bang Records deal. "Right away, Bert brings in Freddie Scott, soon after Van Morrison, who I worked with right up until the time of 'Madame George,'" says Huston. Things were just snowballing. And right around that time I got a call from The Who, who I'd known back in England. And that became *Who Sell Out*."

The year 1967 was, of course, the year of Sergeant Pepper's and psychedelia, the first time pop music was recognized as an 'important' art form. In contrast to the silly self-consciousness of the era, *The Who Sell Out* celebrated the charmingly crass commercialism that was (and still is) pop radio, even including actual radio jingles pilfered from Radio London and original 'mock' ads cooked up by bassist John Entwistle and drummer Keith Moon. 'I Can See For Miles,' recorded at Talentmasters (and various other locales) that July, gave The Who their first foray into the American Top 10. While in New York, the band also completed a backing track for 'Rael,' one of Pete Townshend's earliest extended pieces, in a marathon session that ended well after midnight.

Exhausted, Huston left the building but neglected to put the 'Rael' master reel in storage. Unfortunately, Talentmasters' house janitor then put the tape in the trash. The following morning, a horrified Huston returned to find Townshend's mini-opera doused in cigarette ash and dried soda.

What happened next is the subject of some debate, though the normally reliable Al Kooper, who played organ on the track and was on hand for the follow-up session, recalls that Townshend responded to the news of the 'Rael' ruination by heaving a chair through the control-room glass partition, causing "damage of roughly $12,000." The offending engineer, however, remembers things very differently.

"The intro section of the tape was stretched beyond redemption," says Huston, "but fortunately I had taken home a mono mix of the track the previous evening. So we ended up copying the mono intro onto the master. Pete was pissed off and rightly so. But he did not throw a chair through the control-room window. $12,000? The entire control room didn't cost that much to build – and there was only one pane of ¾-inch glass in the window."

By the end of 1967, Huston had formed a solid work relationship with Berns, who offered to bring the young engineer into the Bang organization full time. But trouble was already afoot. A highly-strung workaholic with a troubled background, Berns had already alienated the Atlantic heads by suing for complete control of the Bang enterprise. On the last week of December, Berns and Huston met over dinner to discuss the future.

"He'd just had a baby, and we were sitting at a table in Mama Leone's, and out of nowhere he says to me, 'Have you ever had a premonition that you were going to die?'" recalls Huston. "Just like that! I was 23 at the time, I was bullet-proof as far as I was concerned. At the office we had this desk that we shared – the drawers on my side were always empty, but his always had a bunch of pill bottles, a gun, stuff like that.

"Shortly after that, I was at home and I got a call from someone informing me that Bert had just passed away from a heart attack. I was stunned – I loved Bert, he was a great guy. We were on the verge of signing our contracts together. Make no mistake,

Bert was a really screwed-up guy – but he also had a wonderful heart." Berns' passing put Huston at a career crossroads, and when an attractive offer came in from the west coast, he took the bait. Over the next several decades, Huston would continue to make great records – only this time it would be from the comfort of his own Los Angeles-based studio.

"The way it used to be was that everyone would have to get together and play together – and there's something completely unique when that happens," says Huston, currently a studio-designer/acoustic-consultant based in Nashville. "That's why those records sound so good! It's not rocket science. The reason why these 'oldies' compare favorably to their technologically superior counterparts is because you're hearing the magic in the room at that session. You know that something exceptional was going in that room if it's a great record. There's no doubt about it! You hear the drums bouncing off the walls, all these different sounds moving and blending together, all these things are happening that you wouldn't put up with in a studio nowadays."

Huston concludes: "I always tell people, 'If the music's right, you don't hear the hiss.' All the technical things that are 'wrong' fall by the wayside. And many times, they actually support the music."

INTERVIEW **AL GORGONI**

Did you really think Veronica was shaking her tush to the fretwork of a dork named Archie? In reality, the cool acoustic guitar heard on the Archies' 1969 smash 'Sugar, Sugar' belongs to a man named Al Gorgoni.

By the time he 'joined' the Archies, Gorgoni had already tracked hundreds of sessions in studios all over New York, helping to pump out the hits for the Coasters, the 4 Seasons and the Shangri-Las.

In 1965, Gorgoni supplied the electric overdub on Simon & Garfunkel's breakout smash 'The Sound of Silence,' then concocted the ethereal guitar backing to Van Morrison's 'Brown Eyed Girl.' And speaking of carefully conceived TV acts, let's not forget Gorgoni's clandestine guitar lines on The Monkees' 'I'm a Believer,' 'A Little Bit Me, A Little Bit You' and many others.

You were on hand when the new generation of producers, writers and artists came along: people like Jeff Barry, Carole King and Barry Mann.
We'd do four sessions a day, same type of music. They'd go with the charts, someone had already chosen the songs, bada-bing, done. After a while, these kids started writing songs for these bubbling-around artists, and we'd go in and get these songs recorded in these

little rooms like Associated. I'd be in there playing electric or acoustic rhythm with the usual rhythm section, drums, electric or upright bass, and so forth. The difference was that the songwriters or artists would just come in with a real basic lead sheet – usually just blocks of chords – and we'd have a look and then be free to submit ideas based on that progression, be it a head arrangement, or an opening riff, whatever. And we'd begin working up a demo this way.

So it started out as mainly demo work?

Generally that was how it went. The artists who were into that more eclectic thing – not Patti Page, but something more hip, R&B – this whole crew was really in a different idiom, it was a fringe kind of thing. What happened is that the artists would go in to do the master take with a different cast of players, but it might not have the same feel that it had on the demo. Eventually the artists starting requesting the people who'd done the demos. That's where people like me, drummer Buddy Salzman, all those guys, came in. And we'd be interchangeable. There'd be me, Hugh McCracken, Vinnie Bell, we'd all cover a lot of ground. Four or five interchangeable rhythm sections that were all really hot. Guys like Chuck Rainey, Eric Gale, and Paul Griffin were a pretty exclusive R&B section, they played a lot together.

How were places like Associated, Dick Charles and Stei-Philips different from the major studios of the time?

The environment in the small studios was a lot more creative, a lot more laid back. Dick Charles was a really small room, as was Allegro. Mira was roomier, you could fit a string section in there with horns and the rhythm section. I used to do a lot of that Barry Mann stuff there, which was a lot more orchestral: Mira was great for that. Stei-Philips could accommodate a string section with a rhythm section. That was Lenny Stei's place on 51st and 7th, right across from 1650 Broadway.

Being in midtown Manhattan, many of these studios were located several flights up in order to escape the noise.

Some had elevators, but a lot of them were walk-ups! You could get a lot of exercise if you were lugging equipment around.

AL GORGONI
Selected discography

THE 4 SEASONS
'Rag Doll'

RUBY AND THE ROMANTICS
'Our Day Will Come'

DIXIE CUPS
'Chapel of Love'

THE SHANGRI-LAS
'Leader of the Pack'

SIMON & GARFUNKEL
'The Sound of Silence'

LOU CHRISTIE
'Lightning Strikes'

THE CYRKLE
'Red Rubber Ball'

THE MONKEES
'I'm a Believer'

NEIL DIAMOND
'Cherry, Cherry'

THE COWSILLS
'The Rain, the Park, and Other Things'

TOMMY JAMES AND THE SHONDELLS
'I Think We're Alone Now'

THE ARCHIES
'Sugar, Sugar'

Which were your favorites?

Phil Ramone's place [A&R], on 48th Street upstairs. You had all the music stores right there, and you also had Jim & Andy's downstairs at the street level, which was a great hang out for musicians. The food was excellent, they let you run a tab and pay it off gradually. It was the kind of place where if you were upstairs at A&R and the trombone player didn't show up, you could always guarantee there'd be someone to replace him waiting downstairs at the bar! A&R was always fun. I remember working with Quincy Jones in there, Bobby Scott, people like that, because Phil had such a great reputation, right from the start. The room was an adequate room – in those days they floated the room, they made sure the soundproofing was up to snuff – but in that case, the magic was Phil.

The 4 Seasons sessions became one of your earliest steady gigs. How did that come about?

I got a call one afternoon from Bob Crewe, who I didn't know at the time. He says, "Al, the date pays $35, can you do it?" I told him fine, and I head down to Mira, and I met Bob at a Frankie Valli session. The song they were working on was 'Sherry.' We cut the track, they sang over it, got it done pretty quickly. It was the bass player, Micky, who came up with the idea to double the bass part in thirds with the guitar.

"And that became part of the sound of that record, along with Frankie's falsetto. Next thing I know, the song became a hit, and I got a call back: they needed to make an album fast. So that was the start. I played on all the hits they had, which lasted quite a while. Most of the time it was Buddy Salzman on drums, though sometimes it might be Gary Chester, with Lou Mauro on bass, Vinnie Bell or Ralph Casale on guitar, and Dave Carey on percussion. Charlie Callelo usually did the arrangements. The first one was at Mira, and we did most of the others four blocks up at Stei-Philips.

With the studios arranged so close together, I imagine you could cover a lot of ground in a single day.

Definitely. You could start at a place like WOR, the old radio studio, where we'd do commercials, jazz dates and the like. That was a great sounding place. I did my first overdub at Olmstead: Connie Francis' 'My Heart Has a Mind of Its Own.' That was upstairs at the Olmstead Building on 40th Street, on the park between 5th and 6th. It was an interesting studio, because the control room was up on the second floor. You had to walk up a flight of stairs to get there, and it looked down on the recording room. Bell was like that. I always thought that was kind of cool.

What about the bigger places like Webster Hall, 30th Street?

I loved Webster Hall, what a great room that was. There were balconies all around, it was beautiful in there, on a par with 30th Street. Like choosing between Babe Ruth and Joe DiMaggio. I also really liked Columbia's 799 7th Avenue studio. Dylan, Miles Davis, a lot of cool stuff was done in there. It felt natural to play in there. They had these half-gobos up between the guys, you could hear really well in there. I broke my toe in there. There was 2x4 nailed to the floor, they were trying to keep some wires tied down, and I was running to get something in between takes and smashed my foot right into the thing. I can still feel that!

In your opinion, what was it that gave these studios their special flavor?

Every place had a hand-made console. That was a big part of it. The sound was homemade! And the resident engineer really knew the board, all its little nuances, and you could hear that on the finished product as well. Unfortunately, house engineers have become a thing of the past.

Do you have any regrets?

When you're in the middle of something like that, of course you don't realize that you'll be looking back on that time as some kind of great period. Had I known that, I would've had even more fun while I was there!

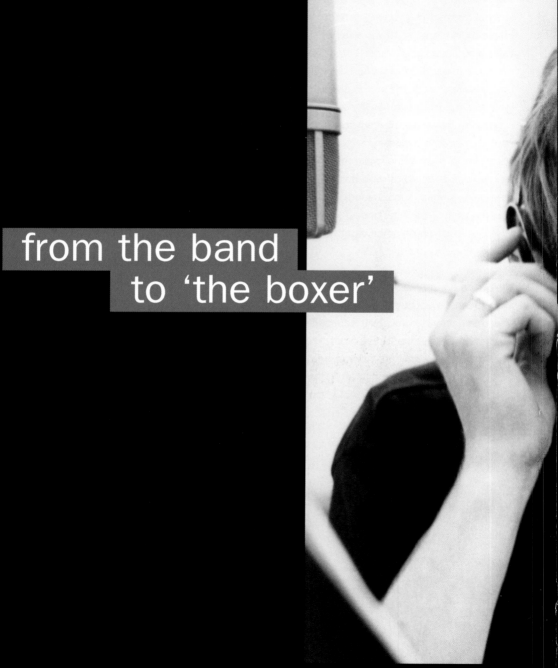

from the band
to 'the boxer'

ape's Skip Spence (left) and Don Stevenson at work on *Wow*, Columbia B at 49 E. 52nd St., late 1967.

n March 1968, Columbia Records continued its rapid evolution with the announcement of a joint venture with Sony of Japan, under the CBS/Sony Records banner. The alliance set the stage for Sony's domination of the world entertainment market (and its eventual purchase of the CBS label, 20 years later). It also coincided with the sale of Columbia Records' longest-running studio, 799 7th Avenue, to Phil Ramone, who re-christened it A&R Number Two shortly after New Year of 1968. It only took weeks for Ramone's new home to create an immediate classic: The Band's legendary *Music From Big Pink*.

"I knew the studio very well from the Columbia days," says John Simon, Big Pink producer. "It was a big studio that had been used by The Lovin' Spoonful, Simon & Garfunkel. That was where we recorded 'The Weight,' 'We Can Talk,' 'Chest Fever,' 'Tears Of Rage' and 'Lonesome Suzie.'"

A&R's distinctive echo chamber (a group of EMT plates in 799's basement eight floors below) was used prominently throughout *Big Pink*. But it turns out that the heavily reverbed drums on 'The Weight' were the result of too few tracks, a drummer who sang and played at the same time, and an engineer who loved leakage.

"We were recording to four track," notes Shelly Yakus, still in his rookie season at the start of 1968. Because of the lack of track space, Yakus – in a style that would become his hallmark – cut the tracks with echo, rather than dubbing it on post-production. "Which meant that if Levon [Helm] sang while he was playing, the vocal and drums went down on the same track, with the same echo," says Yakus, who used an EV-666 on the kick, an Altec 639a for the snare and a Telefunken ELAM for the overhead. "Whatever he sang as lead vocal, that was on the drum track."

In late 1967, shortly before the deal with Ramone was consummated, Columbia packed its gear and relocated to the former site of the CBS Radio Network building at 49 East 52nd Street, a short distance from the CBS 'Black Rock' building, a skyscraper erected in the early 1960s at 51 West 52nd Street. The lead-lined facility consolidated all of CBS Records' operations, with the exception of the ongoing 30th Street Studio. It included a pair of studios (Studio B, on the second floor, and the smaller Studio E upstairs on the sixth floor), with editing rooms on the fourth floor, cutting rooms on the fifth and the company's own research and development staff on the seventh floor.

"What became known as Studio B, the large main studio on the second floor, was the original Arthur Godfrey studio, back when it was CBS radio," says Frank Laico. "We didn't change the place much, just took over the space. Not much needed to be done."

"The fourth floor mixing consoles, like all the consoles at CBS, were custom made in-house by the R&D engineers upstairs," says former CBS staffer Jim Reeves, who engineered the first released multi-track Dolbyed album, *Tom Rush*, produced by Ed Freeman and released on Columbia in 1970. "All the recording engineers would get together with Eric Porterfield, the label's chief R&D engineer and his team, and collaborate on the new console designs for the revamping in 1970," Reeves continues. "They wanted to be absolutely sure that the functionality of their construction efforts would have no shortcomings.

"What differs from how things are manufactured today is that, in the designing stage of these consoles, the recording engineers actually sat with the design staff and communicated what those demands in the modern recording 'process' were, and the consoles were designed to 'make sense' for us as end users. That is part of what made Columbia a world class facility.

"The consoles included Penny & Giles 1dB and 0.5dB per step faders in series per channel, and had 0.5db per step detented rotary faders recessed in the armrest for each input for trims," recalls Reeves. "All channels were preceded by a 20 channel VCA controlled grouped Input Master to adjust overall gain structure. This avoided overloading the summing amps when getting over-enthusiastic with the mix."

In December 1967, Al Kooper recorded his visionary rock-meets-horns project *Child Is Father To The Man*, the debut album from Blood Sweat & Tears, at Studio B. It would be the first of several milestone records to emerge from Columbia's new East 52nd Street facility over the next few years.

LOOKING OUT FOR BIG BROTHER

On the evening of June 18th, 1967, Janis Joplin, a waif-like 24-year-old blues singer who hailed from Port Arthur, Texas, walked on to the stage at the Monterey Pop Festival in California, cued her backing band Big Brother and the Holding Company, and launched into an eight minute blood-and-thunder rendition of Big Mama Thornton's 'Ball and Chain.'

Before she'd even reached the half-way mark, Joplin – dressed in outrageous pink slacks and backed by Sam Andrew's wailing (and slightly out-of-tune) electric – had record company executives salivating and spectator Mama Cass Elliot grinning from ear to ear. "I don't know what happened. I'd never sung like that before," Joplin later recalled. "I just exploded."

Smelling big bucks, management mogul Albert Grossman courted the band and eventually scored a deal with Columbia Records, who bought out the band's contract with the fledgling Mainstream Records label. The following February, Joplin and Big Brother (Sam Andrew, guitar; James Gurley, guitar; Peter Albin, bass; David Getz, drums) arrived in New York and assembled in Columbia's Studio B to begin work on their second LP.

In the control room were producers John Simon and Elliot Mazer, hired by Grossman to capture Big Brother's elemental sound in the studio. "Studio B was cool – a medium sized room, though with no real sound," recalls Mazer. "The control room was typical Columbia: set up for mono. Only the engineer was in the sweet spot. Studio E, upstairs, was smaller and was good for quiet rhythm stuff."

"John and I met out in Detroit to do some live recording of the band at the Grande Ballroom," recalls Mazer. "Afterwards, John decided that he'd start by taking them into the studio in New York for a while, after which I'd record them at Columbia's studio in L.A. for a bit."

Since Big Brother worked best live, Grossman figured that assembling the album (whose working title was *Sex, Drugs And Cheap Thrills*) would be a piece of cake. He figured wrong. "I remember the first time I heard Big Brother, at their premiere at the Anderson Theater in New York," recalls Mazer. "I loved the group. Not everyone shared that opinion, however. That was the thing about Big Brother – their inconsistency could be problematical."

The ramshackle endings, ear-piercing feedback, and perpetually untuned axes were particularly vexing for Simon, who'd put the finishing touches to The Band's *Music From Big Pink* only a month earlier. By June, Simon was beginning to doubt his ability to pull together a listenable album, despite running through an estimated 200 reels of tape.

"John was a skilled musician who graduated from Princeton, had perfect pitch, and could play amazing jazz piano," notes Mazer. "It was definitely more of a challenge for him to work with a band like Big Brother. But I was a rocker. I thought the band's raw energy was amazing. It was just a matter of figuring out the best way to get it down on tape."

On a whim, the Columbia crew decided to try something altogether different. "Janis didn't want to record with earphones," says Mazer, "and the band needed a boost of some sort. So [engineer] Fred Catero rolled out these Altec A7 Voice of the Theater speakers to use as live playback monitors.

"With Janis we had some leakage to contend with, so we mostly used an SM57 for her vocals. Sometimes the entire tonal character of a record comes from leakage – think of all those Andy Johns-Led Zep projects! That became an essential part of the *Cheap Thrills* recording process. The only overdubs were for the extra parts," reports Mazer. "There were no vocal or guitar fixes at all."

The faux-live arrangement set the stage for a monumental rock'n'roll moment. The previous fall, Erma Franklin, sister of soul queen Aretha Franklin, had introduced 'Piece of My Heart,' a searing soul ballad co-written by Atlantic's Bert Berns (author of 'Twist and Shout,' 'Hang On Sloopy,' 'La Bamba' and other three-chord classics).

A proven R&B interpreter, Joplin did not hesitate to dig into the six-month-old tune with reckless abandon, with Andrew and Gurley behind her providing the right amount of controlled mayhem.

"Those guys had these huge Sunn solid-state amps that were like the size of Dual Showmans – just absolutely gnarly-sounding," says Mazer. "But the PA gave the whole thing a real presence. They just filled up the room with this incredible attack. And Janis was right out front, singing live. You can really hear that."

By early summer, advance orders had already pushed the forthcoming Big Brother album into gold-record territory. Columbia's brass demanded that Simon and Mazer tie up the loose ends as soon as possible. "By then we had all these different takes from all the different studios," says Mazer. "Luckily, John has this phenomenal memory – which meant he knew right away that we could take two bars of take 47 of 'Summertime,' and splice it into take 23, and it would sound really good."

Led by the single 'Piece of My Heart' and featuring scorching renditions of 'Ball and Chain' and the Gershwin standard 'Summertime,' *Cheap Thrills* quickly made its way up *Billboard*'s album chart, holding down the top spot throughout the fall of 1968. A million copies had already

> "PEOPLE COME DOWN ON BIG BROTHER FOR THEIR LOOSENESS, BUT SOMETHING HAPPENS ON THAT LIVE RECORD BECAUSE OF THAT. IT'S WHAT MAKES 'CHEAP THRILLS' WORK – BECAUSE YOU CAN'T REHEARSE THE ACCIDENTS."

been sold by the end of September when Grossman announced Joplin's departure from Big Brother. Joplin would go on to make two more albums for Columbia before her untimely demise, in September 1970. But *Cheap Thrills* remains the electrifying pinnacle of her all-too-brief career.

"On the 5.1 version, you can hear Sam and James feeding back, Janis walking around the room with her tambourine. You get a real sense of how this music was made," says Mazer of his SACD re-mix, released in 2001. "People would come down on Big Brother for that looseness, but there's something happening on that record because of that: all these great little accidental moments. That's what makes *Cheap Thrills* work, because you can't rehearse the accidents."

GRAPE EXPECTATIONS

In 1964, producer/engineer David Rubinson was hired by Columbia head Goddard Lieberson to work in the company's classical division. "I spent a lot of time at the 799 7th studio," says Rubinson. "But 30th Street was fantastic, quite simply one of the greatest places I ever worked. I'd been hired by the company to do Broadway cast albums, and all of those albums were cut at 30th Street because of the size of that room – you could put the entire cast of the show in there and record it all live.

"It was just an immense space, with a giant control room as well. It was made for sessions where you had a large, live orchestra, and it was just unbeatable for that type of recording. The main studio itself was kind of L-shaped, so that you could have the chorus in one area, the orchestra on the other, and the lead singers right in the middle."

By the mid-1960s Rubinson was working both coasts for Columbia, and it was during a trip to San Francisco that he signed Moby Grape, a five-man songwriting dynamo and one of the most promising acts to emerge from that spacey summer of 1967. The first triple-guitar threat in rock, the Grape sported lead man Jerry Miller, fingerpicking ace Peter Lewis and, last but not least, Alexander 'Skip' Spence, an off-beat ex-Canadian with an instinct for clever, catchy rock.

When the band's self-titled debut failed to catch on, Rubinson decided to change their surroundings. So, near New Year's 1968, Miller, Lewis and Spence, with drummer Don Stevenson and bassist Bob Mosely, arrived at Columbia's East 52nd Street Studio B, ready to tackle their second album, *Wow*. Spence, author of 'Omaha,' the Grape's only Hot 100 number, imbued the sessions with a warped sense of humor. He dubbed in a hilarious Donald Duck-esque vocal on 'Funky Tunk,' then later added a 1930s-style ditty, 'Just Like Gene Autry; A Foxtrot.' (For added authenticity, on *Wow* the track would only play at 78 rpm.) Upon discovering that the studio was the former home to radio hand Arthur Godfrey, Spence tracked down the old-timer, who supplied the spoken-word intro to Spence's 'Foxtrot.' "The weird thing about that one," recalls Miller, "was that Godfrey actually thought that was the kind of music we did all the time!"

"One thing I remember from those sessions was using reverb from a guitar amp as a chamber," says Rubinson. "We just took a mic-level output and fed it into something like a Fender Princeton reverb, then sent it back out to use for vocals. I did the same thing on the Chambers Brothers and Santana records a short time later. The spring reverbs on those early models had a really nice warm sound, plus you could really control it – there was a depth control, tremolo effect. The only problem was the impedance mismatch, which meant we always had to really pop up the level."

Guitarist Peter Lewis wasn't altogether impressed with the facilities in New York.

"Unlike Elektra or some of the smaller more progressive companies that were innovating their way into the music business at the time, CBS seemed standardized and monolithic," notes Lewis. "The staff producers and engineers at Columbia who I met on both coasts seemed largely the same. For some reason, either company policy or union rules, the CBS engineers were not allowed to push faders past the 0db point. I assume the idea was to prevent distortion at all costs, but for a rock band like Moby Grape, it was sonic death.

"We depended to a huge extent on sounding big and powerful to put our music across, which would have meant saturating the recording tracks with as much signal as much as was humanly possible. Sadly, this didn't happen at Columbia. Although I know there are many people who loved our first record for the songs, etc, there are few who ever heard us live who would say we didn't sound infinitely better in person. But this doesn't get you a hit record.

"Our first record hadn't made us the American Beatles, like everybody thought it would," says Lewis. "By the time we reached New York, we were relatively far down on the food chain at CBS and as a result relegated to the off-hours recording schedule. This meant rolling in around midnight and recording until dawn every night.

"Meanwhile, we were holed up at the Albert or some other flea-bitten hotel, away from our wives and family for months, as the recording process dragged on. One cool thing I do remember, though, is showing up on nights just as some renowned artist would be finishing up. I met Thelonious Monk and Tim Hardin like that. Some of these new friends we even recorded with, people like Mike Bloomfield and Al Kooper."

By that time, Skip Spence's increasingly maniacal personality – intensified by rampant drug use – was beginning to destroy him. Diagnosed with schizophrenia, following a bizarre ax-wielding incident at a Grape recording session that landed him in Bellevue Hospital, Spence exited the Grape, patched together a quirky solo album, *Oar*, a few months later, then gradually slipped into an itinerant world, spending many of the ensuing years in and out of state-assisted mental-health facilities. He passed away in 1999.

BUILDING THE PERFECT BRIDGE

By Paul Simon's own estimation, 1967 was a tough year for Simon & Garfunkel material. "I hit a bit of a dry patch during that period," he later remarked. "Songs like 'A Hazy Shade of Winter' and 'At the Zoo' don't seem that great to me now. In fact, I don't think I regained my stride until about the time of *Bookends* in 1968." To make the most of Simon's impressive new collection of songs, which included 'America,' 'Overs,' and 'Save the Life of My Child', longtime engineering partner Roy Halee was handed the role of producer (in conjunction with S&G) for the second half of *Bookends*.

For Halee – who'd gone from editing classical to recording Dylan just three years earlier – *Bookends* was a major opportunity, and he didn't disappoint, creating the now-familiar multi-textured sound field heard on opening tracks 'Save the Life of My Child' and 'America.'

Released in early April 1968, *Bookends* was a major step forward both musically and sonically. Most importantly, it set the stage for S&G's towering finale, *Bridge Over Troubled Water*, issued in January 1970.

Sessions for *Bridge*, the first important album of the new decade, began in Nashville on November 16th, 1968, with the taping of 'The Boxer.' With Garfunkel involved in the Mike Nichols film *Catch-22*, work effectively ground to a halt for a full year, resuming in November 1969 at Columbia's Studio B at 49 East 52nd Street. By the time *Bridge* was finished so was the career of Simon & Garfunkel, for all intents and purposes. Regardless, *Bridge* would become their crowning achievement, scoring a sea of Grammys and topping album charts the world over (in Britain, it charted for more than 300 weeks, 41 of them at Number One).

INTERVIEW **ROY HALEE**

More than three decades after that work with Simon & Garfunkel, Halee, now a Florida resident, assesses his technical achievement in typically reserved fashion.

Over the years your techniques became progressively more complex – and yet by the time of Bridge Over Troubled Water, Columbia was still operating without 16-track capability.

It's true – I needed a lot of tracks! And Columbia only had eight-track machines in those days. So I devised a way of synching up two eight-track machines to get 16. It was tough, though – you had to hit the record buttons exactly right, or it wouldn't work. I'd do a lot of what we'd call wild tracking, which was just weaving the overdub into the mix later on, often at random.

For example?

The strings at the end of 'The Boxer' are thrown in off a wild mono – same for that little dobro lick that just appears for a second. But the strings kept going out of synch at the end with the voices because the machines were heating up and I couldn't get it to really lock! So I had to mix eight bars, then stop, then mix another eight bars, that sort of thing. As a result, there are lots of edits there. If you could see what went on in an engineering capacity, you wouldn't believe it.

How would you record Paul and Artie's vocal tracks?

Miking the vocals was always a bit of a problem, because a lot of times Artie wanted to do his vocals separately – he always liked to take more time, so he'd say, "I'll do my part later." But whenever I tried doing that, it didn't work, because by isolating them on separate microphones, the blend was never the same. When the two of them were singing live, something would happen in the sound field between their voices and the mic that was magical. That's the way it happened. The minute you'd put a piece of cardboard between them, it went away. So I'd always insist, "You gotta do it live." And we'd get into some pretty heated discussions about it.

Were you double-tracking their vocals?

It's not really doubling, it's more three-quarters original to a quarter overdub. Just to have that second track flesh it out a bit. I'd use a good tube mic, like an old 67, or an M-49. Pretty much those two. Or maybe something else by Neumann, or even a Schoeps on occasion. I've always favored the tube mics – they're more transparent, they're warmer, the harmonic structure seems to be more intact, they're not as analytical. The choice of microphones is really important, obviously, but I was always adamant about keeping everything as clean as possible on the way to the tape machine – the channel, the pre-amp, the whole business.

And, being at Columbia all that time, you certainly didn't lack for console quality.

All the consoles I used at Columbia were crafted in-house, and they were built for dependability, and maybe sacrificed a little bit of transparency. But it didn't matter, they were completely reliable. With the idea being that with 50 or more musicians, you can't afford breakdowns. And they never did – not once. I've been in some studios where the headroom on those pre-amps was so limited, you were always riding by the seat of your pants. Headroom is very important.

What were some of your other favorite rooms around Manhattan?

I loved Mediasound on West 57th: high ceilings, unfinished wood floors, beautiful place. I love ambience – I need to hear that as part of the overall sound. So many of the records that have been done in the years since used these little booths; there's just no character. But what do you expect when you record in a closet? You just aren't going to get any warmth that way. The rooms where I recorded Simon & Garfunkel or the Spoonful – 799 7th Avenue, Studio B at 49 East 52nd Street – were large, they could hold a number of musicians, but they were workable in that they could be deadened if need be, or opened up to get as much ambience as you want. Plus they had a nice reverb time to them.

What sorts of techniques would you use in order to really make the room a part of the record?

I always put ambient mics up. How many depended on the session – there weren't any hard and fast rules. Sometimes you strike out and you don't get it right. You have to experiment. And though you have to have separation in certain instances, I'd always go for leakage. I love it, it makes things sound fuller and more alive. Sure, it's harder to record under those conditions. You have to have an ear for it. And not be afraid of it.

There's some very nice sounding piano on those S&G records, the most celebrated part, obviously, being Larry Knechtel's on 'Bridge Over Troubled Water.'

That came out great, but I'll tell you, piano can be really tough to record. You've got all this phasing going on under the lid, you have to be very careful when you get that close. Classical recordings you don't have that problem, because you're working anywhere from 12 to 18 feet away from a concert grand with the lid open. So you're battling all that. But every pop session I've seen, the mics are right inside the lid, and sometimes the lid's even closed. It's not good. To get around that, I'd always use a third mic in the middle of the piano, and combine that with the other mics. That would usually eliminate a lot of that phasing, with the lid open.

What kind of mics do you use?

It depends. First you have to listen to the piano in the room and how it sounds. I might go with 87s, 67s, 414s, M-49s. But you could use a cheap mic if you wanted a bright sound, you might go with a dynamic mic, like a ribbon mic, a Bauer or Shure. I occasionally might use compression, if you're looking for that sound, but generally I'd start without it. And go from there.

You managed to come up with some pretty extraordinary drum tracks while working with Hal Blaine.

One of my favorites was during the recording of 'Bridge.' I put some tape delay on Hal's bass drum. It was just a creative moment. You know, "I've got this idea, let's just try it, OK?" What you're hearing isn't really what he's actually playing. What he does with his foot is much simpler than that. But with the delay on it, it came out like "Ba-da, ba-da, b-ba-da, ba-da." Neat isn't it? Hal loved it – he said, "Boy, I never would have played it like that!"

On another song, 'The Only Living Boy in New York,' you put his kick drum into the chamber.

It sounds like I did, but that was just a nice accident – the way Hal's kit was miked, there was always a considerable amount of leakage. So what happened is that the bass drum was leaking into another mic that had echo on it. That's what you're hearing – natural leakage, rather than actually applying echo to the bass drum. Because I didn't believe in isolating every single drum, or putting gates on, those things would happen – which was fine with me, because I loved leakage anyway.

Also, I find it very, very distracting to hear drums across a stereo field. If anything, I've just done left-center and right-center. And with room sound around it, using an ambient mic. And in a lot of cases, straight mono. Very often, the drums don't sound as big if they're placed across the stereo field. There's not that natural balance. I mean, would you want to go in and do a big-band date and have the toms swishing from left to right? Which you hear all the time, it's crazy. I think you get in trouble once you split drums like that.

Like Frank Laico, you turned echo into an art form.

If you loved echo, you couldn't top Columbia, they had the best rooms for echo around. 30th Street, of course, was famous for its live chambers, Studio B had a chamber as well, and there was the great stairwell over at Studio A. Unfortunately, you don't see many live chambers any more – it's all pretty much digitally reinforced reverb, rather than staircases, bathrooms and live rooms. I think live echo is kind of a lost art.

There's a fairly well-known story about how you guys got that "really big voice" for 'The Only Living Boy in New York.'

For the middle section of that song, Art had suggested a multitude of vocal tracks cobbled together, with a subtle harshness added as well. It was simply another case of creative engineering. I put them right into the echo chamber! Because Columbia had great echo chambers, I said let's just mic it right in there, let's not even add the echo after. So that's what we did. Natural reverb. I couldn't get an airy, bright quality to it at first in the EQ, so I ended up using Dolby on it, without resolving the Dolby. And what a great sound. Of course, it was hotter than hell in there!

What other homemade devices would you use?

I loved to put guitar amps in bathrooms and halls, placing one mic right in front of the amp and another down the hall – or two if you wanted stereo – and combine them in the mix. If you do it just right you can create the kind of ambient sound that you just couldn't get out of a box.

If you could name one defining characteristic to describe your recording style, what would that be?

I've always tried to go into any session without any pre-conceived ideas. Once the session was underway, I'd just try to shape the sound in as imaginative a way as possible. Believe me, things didn't always work out that great – but I hope it was always done in good taste, anyway.

RECORDING 'THE BOXER'

Several months and more than 100 hours of studio time in the making, 'The Boxer,' released as a single in April 1969, was to Simon & Garfunkel what 'Good Vibrations' had been to Brian Wilson three years earlier: a landmark recording and a commercial, artistic, and technical triumph.

Recorded in numerous facilities in both Nashville and Manhattan (including Columbia University's beautifully ambient chapel), 'The Boxer' featured such disparate instrumentation as lap steel, bass harmonica, dobro, and piccolo trumpet – and, for a finishing touch, one of the most famous percussion overlays in history.

The song began with a basic acoustic-guitar with percussion rhythm track, recorded in short order at Columbia's Music Row studios in November 1968 with country session guitarist Fred Carter, Jr. (who concocted the song's distinctive opening flourish). Back in New York, however, the spirit of technical creativity that marked the classic *Bookends* sessions took over.

"Once Paul and Artie hooked up with me, they wanted to start doing things in a tastier way," remembers producer Halee. "Especially after they finally had the clout to make it happen, after *Bookends* and 'Mrs. Robinson.' That's when [Columbia head] Clive Davis gave me my own studio out in San Francisco to do whatever I wanted there. Unfortunately, I ended up going to L.A. all the time, because those guys were there."

Among "those guys" was drumming pro Hal Blaine, who wound up tagging along with Halee one quiet weekend in New York, his 'big drums' in tow. Eventually Blaine found himself standing alongside an elevator shaft in the CBS building in an effort to fulfill Halee's love of big, natural reverb.

"There we were with all these mic cables, my drums, and a set of headphones," says Blaine. "When the chorus came around – the 'lie-la-lie' bit – I came down on my snare as hard as I could. In that hallway, right next to this open elevator shaft, it sounded exactly like a cannon shot! Which was just the kind of sound that we were after in the first place."

The middle section of 'The Boxer' is a story unto itself. For starters, Simon hadn't even conceived a solo break for his song; that honor, strangely enough, belongs to the largely non-composing Art Garfunkel, who'd heard the moving melody line in his head one afternoon and suggested using it as an instrumental passage. So impressed was Simon that he ended up ditching an additional verse – "I am older than I once was, and younger than I'll be" – to make room for his friend's invention. (The 'discarded' verse would re-appear from time to time in various Simon/S&G live renditions.)

The solo itself, like everything else on 'The Boxer,' was recorded in typically unconventional fashion. In Nashville, during the song's early stages, session wizard Pete Drake was summoned to cut a pedal steel interpretation of Garfunkel's melody. But it was back in Manhattan weeks later that the passage would take on its unique character.

During that time, Simon & Garfunkel were checking out a chapel on the campus of Columbia University as a possible location for a forthcoming Christmas television special. The natural ambience of the building was so compelling, in fact, that the duo decided then and there to cut the yet-to-be-completed vocal overdubs for 'The Boxer' as a remote recording.

Somewhere during the course of hauling mics and mixers in and out of the house of worship came the idea of taping a wind instrument for use in the solo section. Eventually the call went out for a piccolo trumpeter – and Halee insists it had nothing to do with the Beatles' 'Penny Lane'. Yet rather than choose one part over the other, Halee – in yet another creative flash – decided to make a single dub of the two diverse instruments. Back in his CBS control room on 52nd Street, the producer carefully melded Tennessee country with New York classical, and the now-famous passage was complete.

Not everyone could see its future relevance at the time. On more than one occasion Halee was forced to placate CBS boss Clive Davis, who'd wondered aloud, "Why do you have to go to a *church*? Why don't you just do it in a *studio*?"

from funk
to punk

The start of a new decade coincided with a major shift in the sound of black American music. In the spring of 1970, James Brown recruited young bassist Bootsy Collins and cut a strident new single, 'Get Up (I Feel Like Being Like a Sex Machine).' Stripped to the bone and achingly rhythmic, the repeating groove of 'Sex Machine' included all the essential elements of the emerging funk culture, and became the blueprint for nearly every dance hit to follow.

In New York, Sylvester Stewart – aka Sly Stone – was busy doing his own thing from inside Columbia's East 52nd Street Studio B. Growing up in San Francisco's Bay Area, Stewart came of age listening to both gospel and the Beatles. Graduating from DJ to record producer by age 19, he quickly learned his way around the recording studio and was soon cutting hits for Bobby Freeman ('The Swim'), the Beau Brummels ('Laugh, Laugh,' 'Just A Little') and other San Francisco acts.

In 1966, Stewart enlisted the support of siblings Freddie and Rosie, cousin Larry Graham, and high school chums Jerry Martini, Greg Errico, and Cynthia Robinson to launch the multi-racial, multi-musical Sly and the Family Stone. The title of the group's first Epic album – *A Whole New Thing* – said it all: mixing R&B vocals with pop horns over a rock backbeat, the Family Stone really was like nothing else in pop music at the end of the 1960s.

In 1968, the group scored with 'Dance to the Music,' a distillation of Stone's stylistic influences to date (featuring fuzz bass, doo-wop harmony and, of all things, a Klezmer clarinet). Stewart made the most of his versatile crew by writing a collection of songs – among them 'Stand,' 'Everyday People,' 'Hot Fun In The Summertime' – that were infectious, melodic, rhythmic, and complex. On the group's pivotal fourth album, *Stand!*, Stewart helped redefine the role of R&B guitar. 'Thank You (Falettinme Be Mice Elf Agin),' the single that followed, underscored Sly's genius, and remains the single greatest one-chord hit in history. ·

"Sly was totally revolutionary," remarks ex-CBS producer/engineer Don Puluse, the man behind the console for the majority of the Family Stone's hit parade. "He had a whole different way of working things out in the studio. Sly would relay the ideas and I'd make them happen in the control room. Because back then, of course, you couldn't touch the console if you weren't union. Which, in a way, worked to our advantage – with someone like Sly around, it made us engineers work that much harder, just to prove how good we really were."

Puluse remembers putting the finishing touches on 'Sing a Simple Song,' a stand-out track from *Stand!,* at 30th Street Studio of all places, taking full advantage of the church's big live chambers in the process.

"We did some of the vocals at the church," says Puluse, "though not in the huge room, but in the little sacristy that they'd turned into a separate recording room. I loved that track! It was funny – during the recording of Sly's lead vocal, I looked up, and right at the part where you hear that little scream in the chorus, he was running from one side of the room to the other! Which is exactly what it sounds like on the record! We just mimicked him running from left to right by panning his vocal right across, with added reverb. But Sly was always full of that kind of stuff."

WONDER YEARS

In 1971, Motown's resident boy genius, Stevie Wonder, was on a creative roll. On his 21st birthday, Wonder gained access to the accumulated song royalties held in trust from self-penned hits like 'I Was Made to Love Her' and 'My Cherie Amour.' On the same day, his contract with Motown expired. For Wonder, the combination of financial and artistic freedom was a powerful weapon.

Rather than immediately re-sign with Motown, Wonder dipped into his cash reserves and outfitted his New York apartment with a full-service recording studio, then began writing. And writing. At a Motown meeting later that year, Wonder stunned executives with a small sampling of his bounty – 'Superwoman,' 'Tuesday Heartbreak,' 'You've Got It Bad Girl,' among others – then quickly negotiated a new deal that included a handsome royalty increase as well as the establishment of his own publishing wing.

But the most important piece of the puzzle fell into place when Wonder retained the services of producer/engineer Robert Margouleff and his partner, Malcolm Cecil, synth-programming wizards whose experimental collection *Zero Time*, in the guise of Tonto's Expanding Head Band, had caught Wonder's fancy. Over the next 24 months, Wonder, with help from Margouleff and Cecil, would assemble a body of work that was arguably the most consistent stretch of pop-music making by any artist since the Beatles.

Though the prolific Wonder could afford to give away future hits like 'Tell Me Something Good' (to Rufus) and 'Until You Come Back To Me' (to Aretha Franklin), both million sellers, at the last minute he decided to recall a gritty funk track originally intended for guitarist Jeff Beck. Written in one night in the summer of 1972, and issued later that year, 'Superstition' would become Wonder's first Number One pop smash since his debut single, 1963's 'Fingertips – Part 2,' and light a fire under his solo career.

Of the four inter-connecting albums issued through the period – *Music of My Mind, Talking Book, Innervisions,* and *Fufillingness' First Finale* – for Margouleff, 1972's *Talking Book* remains the top of the heap.

"It was the culmination of everything that Malcolm and I had brought to Stevie up to that point," says Margouleff. "*Music of My Mind* was a beginning, but by *Talking Book*, things had really solidified. The ideas were still flowing, we were doing a lot of really creative things on the tracks, such as modifying the inner workings of Steve's clavinet and using guitar boxes on the keyboards. And of course all of the synthesizer programs we'd developed were still very fresh. That album meant everything to us. Whenever I flew out to L.A. from New York to work on the record, I'd always keep the tapes right there on my lap – that's how attached I was to it."

Most of the album's rhythm tracks were assembled at Electric Lady Studios on West 8th Street in lower Manhattan. The former home of the Village Barn, a popular big-band venue during the 1940s and 1950s, the Greenwich Village building had been purchased in 1968 as a real-estate investment by Jimi Hendrix – who initially considered turning the space into a rock club.

Completed shortly before Hendrix's death in November 1970, Electric Lady included a pair of street-level studios, with office space and living quarters on the second and third floors respectively. Outside, a curved-brick façade gave the studio an air of distinction. In 1997, the building's new owner incurred the wrath of neighbors and historians alike by replacing the façade with a sterile glass front.

"Electric Lady was designed to give an atmosphere of being in space," wrote Hendrix associate Curtis Knight, "featuring every electronic innovation that could be conceived." Among the list of leading-edge devices was a 32-track recording facility – no small feat in 1970.

The surplus of track space was tailor-made for the multi-talented Wonder, who covered all basic instrumental chores single-handedly. "Steve's an excellent drummer," says Margouleff. "A lot of those songs would start out with Steve just laying down a nice steady rhythm part. That was how 'Superstition' was cut – everything but the horns were done right there in one night, from dusk till dawn. We'd set up all the instruments in the studio in a sort of semi-circle, with everything always up and running so Steve could easily move from one part to the next without having to wait."

With its arid drums, swirling keyboards and crystalline, up-front vocals, *Talking Book* was unlike any other work produced for Motown, a label known for its massive, echo-laden production style. "Their stuff was always big bombast, whereas this was very immediate," says Margouleff. "Reverb is often used to create a sense of space and depth, but in this case, we wanted a 'touchable' kind of sound, which is what the term 'talking book' implies. It just felt better drier."

When echo was applied, Margouleff made certain that it didn't detract from the intimacy of the recording. "Whereas most echo sends will take a mono signal on one side and return it in stereo, we used totally discreet chambers and effects for each side – so that if a conga playing on the left side had reverb on it, the effect appeared *behind* the signal, rather than splashed to the other channel. Which is part of the reason why *Talking Book* has that remarkable clarity throughout."

Though a somewhat unusual choice for miking vocals, Margouleff found the Electro-Voice RE-20 to be particularly well-suited to Wonder's performance style. "We tried a few other mics, but for that close, intimate kind of sound, the RE-20 was really the perfect mic," notes Margouleff. "Because it's a very directional mic, Steve was able to find its axis quite easily – plus he could sing right up against the windscreen without having to worry about pops or anything."

Given the sheer volume of songs in Wonder's collection at the time – and since he couldn't read from a lyric sheet – some assistance was required when it came time to cut the lead vocals. "There were just tons and tons of words, and at the point Steve was writing songs so fast he couldn't possibly memorize everything," recalls Margouleff.

> "WE CUT 'SUPERSTITION' IN A NIGHT, FROM DUSK TO DAWN, WITH THE INSTRUMENTS SET IN A SEMI-CIRCLE SO STEVIE COULD MOVE EASILY BETWEEN THE PARTS."

"So when he needed help, we'd just feed him the words, line by line, right there while he was recording the track! Malcolm [Cecil] would be in the control room over the talkback, guiding him through his headphones, a few bars ahead: 'You are the sunshine of my life … You are the apple of my eye,' and so forth. If you listen real carefully, you can actually hear a little of Malcolm through the headphone leakage!"

As a crowning touch, crossfades were used in place of the traditional three-second track gap, which transformed *Talking Book* into one seamless body of music. "That was Malcolm's concept," says Margouleff. "We wanted the album to stand as a single entity, rather than as a collection of songs. The thing is, those crossfades aren't individual edits – we physically put them there all at once. After we had all the mixes finished, we just played back the whole record, manually adding each of the crossfades right there at the console. We actually rehearsed the whole thing a few times. Of course, that concept would later become the backbone of the disco movement – but we really invented it."

Issued shortly after Wonder's triumphant summer tour with the Rolling Stones, *Talking Book* became an immediate crossover smash, soaring into the Top Five on the strength of back-to-back Number One hits 'Superstition' and 'You Are the Sunshine of My Life.' Though *Talking Book* – as well as the monumental works that followed – presented Wonder as a serious album artist for the first time in his career, it would take some time for the public to catch on. Despite a host of hit singles and Grammy accolades, not one of Wonder's 1970s albums would achieve gold-record status. He does however remain the fourth best-selling singles artist of all time.

"Along with the production assistance, Malcolm and I were able to keep Steve on track, to help him focus on all this amazing material that was pouring out of him on a daily basis," says Margouleff, who also snapped the indelible portraits of Wonder that grace the front and back covers of *Talking Book*. "It was an incredible gift to be there, to be part of something that changed the course of popular music – and that changed my life as well."

BAPTISM OF FUNK

Funk was in full force by the early 1970s, and New Jersey's Kool & the Gang were well-positioned to ride the wave. Led by bassist Robert 'Kool' Bell and his horn-playing brother Ronald, the versatile Jersey City outfit spent the previous decade working jazz dates with the likes of Pharoah Saunders before morphing into one of New York's hottest live R&B acts. Still, crossover success remained elusive, and as the summer of 1973 unfolded, the brothers Bell, and Gang associates George Brown (drums), Claydes Smith (guitar), Dennis Thomas (flute/sax), Ricky Westfield (keyboards) and Robert Mickens (trumpet), made preparations to record a sixth album, determined to change their luck. Incredibly, it would take just one night to lay the groundwork for the songs that would last them a lifetime.

The Gang's studio-of-choice was Mediasound Recording Studio, located in midtown at the corner of 8th Avenue at 311 West 57th Street. A stately facility that had once been the site of the Manhattan Baptist Church, Mediasound had, by the early 1970s, become one of the most popular recording establishments in the city. "They'd left things pretty much intact from the church days," says veteran producer/engineer Jeffrey Lesser,

■ **ROY HALEE (producer)** "Mediasound on West 57th Street was probably my favorite studio in all of New York. It had these really high ceilings, old wooden floors with no finish whatsoever – there was a lot of wood in that place. Acoustic instruments sounded fabulous in there, and you could do everything from a string quartet to a rock session – there aren't too many studios that can make that claim. It was a truly amazing place."

who'd joined the studio's engineering staff a few years earlier. "They took out the pews, of course, and put up this burnt-cork insulation on the ceiling. But the stained glass was still there, so was the organ loft – it was just a beautiful place. Studio A had a really nice-sounding API board, with an eight-track unit at first and then 16, with a short-lived 12-track in between."

It was Mediasound's smaller, pentagon-shaped Studio B, located one flight down, that saw the bulk of the Kool & the Gang action. "It was definitely a lot drier and more intimate in that room," notes Lesser, "and the band really could get a good groove going down there because they were playing right next to each other, with very little baffling."

As Lesser recalls, 'Funky Stuff,' 'Jungle Boogie' and 'Hollywood Swinging' – the centerpiece for club classic *Wild and Peaceful* – began as simple jams without form. "I'd never really experienced anything quite like it," says Lesser of his work with the Gang. "I'd start recording, and they'd usually just get grooving on one chord, maybe switch a chord here and there, but keep it pretty constant, and this would go on for the duration of the session. Then Ronald would go home with the rough mixes, return the next day, and we'd start editing these different grooves together. From there he'd start to write a song that would include the groove with the chords, editing the chord changes back in. He had this vision, even while they were just jamming – and he'd take the essence of it and just carve it away like a sculptor, until he had a completed song. It was really something to watch evolve."

Intuitively, Lesser put a premium on the rock-bottom rhythms of drummer Brown, and the results were often startling.

"On 'Funky Stuff,' the main groove was accentuated by this big, open floor-tom beat," says Lesser, who used a 57 on the snare, Neumann 87s on the toms and a 421 on the kick. "My assistant engineer, who went on to be a very famous and successful mixer, did the mic set-up. We got this fantastic take of the song, and afterwards I really wanted to highlight the sound of that floor tom. So I'm bringing it up and up in the mix, but no matter what I did it still sounded too room-y and I couldn't get it focused. The thing is, the band loved it, they kept saying, 'How did you do that? It's great!' Later I went out to check a few things, and there was that 87 over the floor tom in cardioid position – with the live side facing the wrong way! On the one hand, I was totally embarrassed – but it was because we did it *wrong* that they ended up with that sound! Incredible."

Though the majority of the band tracks were done live, no song was complete without the obligatory 'party' overdub, complete with festive whistles and ad-libbed vocals, which Lesser treated with a generous coating of church-like echo. "That was mostly plate reverb from one of the early EMT 140 models we had there, which was about 10 feet long and a foot wide," says Lesser. "It was big and warm, with a little meter and a few red buttons and dampers on the inside that allowed you to set the length of the decay just by physically matting it down. And we definitely stuck a little tape slap with the reverb."

In August, the single 'Funky Stuff' gave the Gang its first-ever Top 30 pop hit. But that was just a warm-up for the audacious 'Jungle Boogie,' which wound up reaching the Top Five on both pop and R&B charts. The following spring, 'Hollywood Swinging' became yet another gold single and the band's premier R&B Number One.

> **"'ROCKAWAY BEACH' WAS IN THE TRADITION OF THE BEST QUEENS-BRED POP, A KISSING COUSIN TO THE SOUND AND SPIRIT OF THE SHANGRI-LAS."**

Though the group would later become a major hit-making force during the 1980s, albeit on significantly less-funky material, *Wild and Peaceful* remains the definitive Kool & the Gang effort, even 30 years on.

"People sometimes think these things are manicured and manipulated," says Lesser, who went on to record Lou Reed's *New York* album as well as a slew of recent efforts by The Chieftains. "When in reality, they just ran in there, played the song, ran out, and that was it. There's a different kind of energy when you're working fast and live like that … and as a result, the songs became great."

ONE, TWO, THREE, FOUR!

Only 20 years had passed since Elvis Presley arrived with his first volley of 1950s hits, but the world he departed in August 1977 was a much-changed place. Rock'n'roll, once the mouthpiece of the working-class, had become the preferred flavor of the coke-sniffing rich. In New York's trendy uptown nightclubs, the infectious grooves of early-1970s funk had been replaced by the robotic rhythms of disco, at 120 beats per minute. On the charts, Debbie Boone capped an unctuous year in pop with 'You Light Up My Life,' holding down the Number One spot for 10 excruciating weeks, while soft-rockers like Dan Fogelberg, Dan Hill, and England Dan & John Ford Coley ruled FM with tales of unrequited love.

At the end of a turbulent Big Apple summer marked by a garbage strike, a massive blackout, and a ritualistic murderer who took orders from a dog, the Ramones, a black-clad rock quartet from Queens who all answered to the same last name, entered Mediasound Studio. They were there to begin work on *Rocket To Russia*, a third album for Sire Records.

A triumphant tour of the U.K. the previous year had established the Ramones (guitarist Johnny, vocalist Joey, bassist Dee Dee and original drummer Tommy) as the leading purveyors of punk and the first palpable response to the effete perfectionism of 1970s rock. For the Ramones and the rest of punk-rock nation, 1977 was a watershed year, one that included the release of pivotal works, from the Dead Boys' *Young Loud & Snotty* to the Sex Pistols' infamous *Never Mind the Bollocks Here's the Sex Pistols.* While frontmen Stiv Bators (Boys) and Johnny Rotten (Pistols) personified the most abrasive elements of the genre, on stage and in the studio the Ramones' weapon was the loud, fast (and barely) two-minute pop song.

In late August, hoping to catch the last rays of summer, the band recorded 'Rockaway Beach,' Joey Ramone's ode to a favored seaside hangout. A volley of monstrously distorted barre chords supporting a melody that nicked a handful of surf-rock themes, 'Rockaway Beach,' like its predecessor, 'Sheena is a Punk Rocker,' was in the tradition of the best Queens-bred pop, a kissing cousin to the sound and spirit of the Shangri-Las (who, ironically, launched a comeback that summer at CBGB, The Bowery's punk haven).

Though it failed to crack the Top 40, at Number 66 'Rockaway Beach' became the first significant single from a band that had but one mission: to give the rock establishment a long overdue kick in the ass.

Despite the overseas success of staples 'Pinhead' and 'Blitzkrieg Bop' – both building-blocks for an entire generation of British punks – domestic record sales remained sluggish. "Right before we went in to do *Rocket To Russia*, Johnny played me a copy of the Pistols' 'God Save The Queen,'" recalls Ed Stasium, a guitarist-turned-studio engineer who'd arrived in time to help the band record its second effort, *The Ramones Leave Home*. He knew the Pistols had basically copied their sound from the Ramones – and he wanted to prove that the Ramones were capable of doing something a whole lot better.

In an effort to capture the full-tilt energy of the band's rhythm section once and for all, the crew abandoned New York's ultra-dry Sundragon Studios and relocated to the abundantly ambient Mediasound, by 1977 one of Manhattan's most favored recording sites.

"Media was an amazing place – it was huge," says Stasium. "They kept the tall ceilings in there, which must have been about 130 feet high. And you could get an absolutely killer drum sound in there, it was the best place in all of New York for that. We could do everything in there – recording, mixing, you name it." An association with audio ace Roy Thomas Baker several years earlier had taught Stasium a thing or two about the importance of getting the room into the big picture. "I'd been accustomed to tight-miking everything, you know? Pad up the walls, pad up the drums. But then I went to work with Roy who said, 'Hey, we need some room sound in here!' And he pulled the mic back 20 feet from the drums. So when I got to do *Rocket to Russia*, I still had the drums tight-miked, but it was also the first time I'd really miked up the room, using some 87s, and recorded to two separate tracks in stereo."

That tight/ambient combo proved positively explosive on *Rocket to Russia*'s opening salvo of 'Cretin Hop' and 'Rockaway Beach.' "Talk about a drum room – that place had the most killer sound in all of New York!" says Stasium. "We had Tommy playing wide open in the middle of the room, I just baffled off Johnny's amplifiers, and I put Dee Dee in a room in the back down by the bathroom."

Unlike the Ramones' wham-bam first two efforts, *Rocket to Russia* was an uncharacteristically detailed affair that derived its massive sound from piles of overdubbed guitar tracks. "Where *Ramones Leave Home* had been done very quickly and with hardly any pre-production at all," says Stasium, "*Rocket to Russia* was where we really started going for a much more streamlined sound. We had all kinds of guitar sounds – acoustic, clean guitars – that's when it really started happening. The thing is, we still wanted it to sound live!"

When all else failed, says Stasium, "John just turned all of the knobs on his Marshall up to 10."

Unfortunately, radio programmers fixated on the 'clean' sounds of Southern California weren't about to give an inch to a band of four-chord scrubs from the boroughs. At No. 49, *Rocket to Russia* was the Ramone's most commercially successful album to date, though hardly the major breakthrough they'd been hoping for. But within a year, bands like the Cars, the Knack and various new wave flavors-of-the-month were riding all the way to the bank on a sound perfected by the brothers Ramone. The irony was way too thick for drummer Tommy.

"Dey say our music's stoopid," he complained. "Whadda dey want? Fer us to use flugel horn 'n' strings, or sumtin'?"

INTERVIEW **ED STASIUM**

Raised in New Jersey and schooled on the streets of Manhattan, producer Ed Stasium was immediately snared by the magic of New York pop radio of the 1960s; by the end of that decade, Stasium himself was playing guitar and keyboards and fronting his own band, Men Working (later re-born as Brandywine). Signed to the Brunswick label, Stasium got an early appreciation for the funkiness of the urban studio environment when his band arrived at New York's Allegro Recording Studio (home to the Lovin' Spoonful and birthplace of innumerable "bubblegum" hits) for a first-ever pro recording session, before moving on to the majestic Mediasound Studio. "My first really cool recording experience," notes Stasium.

By the early 1970s, Stasium was out of Brandywine but still into the idea of record making. Back in Jersey, he took a job as an apprentice engineer at Venture Sound, the start of a fruitful relationship with producer Tony Bongiovi, cousin to 1980s pop idol Jon Bon Jovi. In the summer of 1976, Bongiovi asked Stasium to help record the second effort by a scruffy quartet from Queens named The Ramones. For Stasium, it was a case of right place, right time.

With The Ramones spearheading the world-wide punk phenomenon, Stasium became immediately identified with the tough, Big Apple-based sound, a reputation solidified by his work on Talking Heads' debut, *Talking Heads: 77*, as well as his first full-fledge production credit, The Ramones' legendary *Road To Ruin* (which also featured Stasium on guitars and bass).

By the turn of the 1980s, Stasium was an independent, expanding his musical palate to include artists like Mick Jagger, Carly Simon, and Julian Cope. His work on Living Colour's multiplatinum *Vivid* and *Time's Up*, along with the Smithereens' *11* and *Blow-Up*, Motorhead's *1916*, and Marshall Crenshaw's *Life's Too Short* helped make "the Stasium sound" one of the most audible production styles of the late 1980s and early 1990s.

You started out in this business as a guitarist, fronting your own band and actively writing songs. That must have had some bearing on your approach once you got on the other side of the glass?

There are some producers who are more 'vibe' guys – they create a great vibe in the studio. It isn't even about the sound, per se, because they've got their engineers to do that. Me, I tend to crawl into the songs a little more than some other guys, even though I don't profess to ever having been a major songwriter. But it allows me the latitude to say something like, "Why don't we take this bridge out and put something else in there."

Which is like the George Martin method – making physical changes to the music when necessary.

But then again they might turn right around and say, "No, we liked it better they other way!" The point is that two-way communication is really a big part of the recording process. For me, it's because of my musical background, but it's also because I'm a big fan. It's just second-nature to me, the same instinct that tells me to turn a knob on the console up 7K.

You've worked with such a wide range of artists – Ramones, Peter Wolf, Living Colour, Talking Heads. Does your technical approach vary from album to album?
Though I kind of set up everything the same way technically speaking, I still have to take each project by the horns. If it's a more laid-back songwriter type, obviously I'll ease up a bit. But if someone comes to me and says, "Hey, we need something else here, but we don't know what it is," that's when I'll come out and give them some of my own suggestions – still bearing in mind that I want it to sound like it's their record, not mine.

Your 'suggestions' tend to be on the heavier side of the sound spectrum. Marshall Crenshaw's Life's Too Short, for instance, really benefited from such beefiness.
I know – that was a pretty 'big' record, especially for a guy like Marshall. But it's not like I planned it that way!

Your style had become quite distinctive by the time of the Living Colour and Smithereens sessions. 'Cult of Personality,' 'A Girl Like You' – those are huge-sounding records. What were you doing?
Mostly that's just compressed room sound, maybe a little 'verb on there as well. But I also used the old gated-plate trick – I took the snare track, put it on its own channel, gated it severely, and then sent it through an old EMT plate or an AMS RMX reverb. Still, it's mostly the room sound. Though on [the Smithereens'] 'A Girl Like You,' I emphasized the drum hits during the mixes using automation, you know, where Dennis [Diken] would come down on that part of the riff – da-da-da-da-da ... POW! It just pushes up the reverb, the room, everything right on that downbeat.

It's probably difficult for Ramones listeners to believe those records were cut in a church.
I know, but it's true. We could do everything in there – recording, mixing. Eventually we took the stuff over to Power Station to mix once it was half-way together. At that point, Power Station had literally nothing for effects – no reverb, no plates, and this was just before digital came in. But there was this great hallway on the east side of the building, so I just put some speakers and microphones down there, and used it as an echo chamber. In fact they still use it that way now that it's Avatar – they've probably still got the same mics and speakers I put up!

Early on, were there any experiences in particular that helped shape your career as a producer?

I remember working with [Queen producer] Roy Thomas Baker, recording the band Pilot at Quebec's Morin Heights. Prior to that, everything I did was based on the 'dead' sound – you know, carpeting, padding, taping things down, and of course tight-miking everything. Then along comes Roy, looks at my set-up and says, "Hey, what about the *room*?" And I'm going, "Room sound, what are you talking about?" [laughs] So from that point forward, my goal was to always try to get the sound of the recording room. I started pushing the mics way back, just to get those acoustics in there. And that became my main technique.

And you did that with the Ramones' records?

Yeah, that was the first time, in fact. I still close-miked, but I got the sound of that Media room in there as well.

And you had quite a room to work with there.

I know. I mean, I didn't use much of it, but you can hear it.

Those Ramones records certainly don't sound fussed-over. Did you do any pre-production?

The Ramones Leave Home, their second album, went really quick, without any pre-production at all, although *Road to Ruin* took a very long time to record. Then again, pre-production with the Ramones was often a matter of getting into the studio and going, "Let's try this, let's try that." Or Johnny saying to me, "I wannit to sound like dis, but I can't do it like dat, so you do it, Eddie!" [laughs.] That sort of thing.

I think a lot people take for granted how great Johnny's guitar sounds on those records – they don't realize how easy it is to take a potentially big-sounding guitar and make it small, if you're not careful.

If it sounds good coming out of the amp, there shouldn't be a problem. Then again, you hear about people spending a couple weeks on the guitar sounds. Then a few months on the drums! "Hey, OK, we finished the drums, we're ready!" I think that's silly – it's not like it's brain surgery.

You have a reputation for layering, rather than just going in there and getting the takes quickly.

I always layer stuff, being from the Roy Thomas Baker school. You know, I'll double-track guitars and do a lot of different parts, rather than just going out there and recording a band live: "OK, that's sounds good, let's go, boom." That's one approach, but I personally like to sculpt the records that I make.

Even those Ramones records?

Sure – we were double-tracking on *Ramones Leave Home*, and by the time of *Rocket to Russia* we had all kinds of guitar sounds – acoustic, clean guitars – that's when it started happening. And *Road to Ruin* had tons of overdubs.

It sure sounds live.

But that's the way we wanted them to sound! 'Rockaway Beach,' 'Sheena is a Punk Rocker,' it's not like there were multiple guitars split dead left and right, but there was always at least another guitar under there, just to thicken it, to add a little extra spiff to it. 'I Wanna Be Sedated' has lots of guitars – Johnny's playing his, then I'm in there with my Strat, doing that "dit-dit-dit-dit" rhythm thing, muting the chords, as well as that one-note solo.

You're doing that solo on 'Sedated'?

Yeah. I figured if Neil Young could do it, I could too!

if i can
make it there

Between the flash of disco and the thrash of punk, the late 1970s offered little room for the popular vocal acts who had dominated the charts during the previous two decades. Tony Bennett's 22-year affiliation with Columbia Records had come to a halt; though still popular on the concert circuit, Dean Martin, Sammy Davis Jr. and many other crooners from the past had long since conceded the airwaves to the rock crowd.

Things weren't looking much brighter for the Chairman of the Board, Frank Sinatra, as the 1970s came to a close. Six years had elapsed since his last studio effort, *Some Nice Things I've Missed*, an album that sported 'nice' material like Jim Croce's 'Bad, Bad Leroy Brown' (done bad, badly) and other half-hearted attempts at staying current. At 65, Ol' Blue Eyes' record-making days appeared to be over for good.

As he prepared to mark his 40th year as a recording artist, Sinatra, with producer-sidekick Don Costa, laid out an idea for a three-part concept album entitled *Trilogy*, covering selections from the old days, the modern era, and the 'future' (featuring symphonic impressions by longtime arranger Gordon Jenkins). Included in the 'present' segment was the theme song from the 1977 film *New York, New York*, Martin Scorcese's over-long jazz-era drama that starred Liza Minnelli and Robert DeNiro. Minnelli's rendition, issued as a single shortly after the film's debut, died a quick death; nonetheless, over the next two years 'Theme from *New York, New York*' became a regular part of her live shows. Sinatra heard it, liked it, and decided it fitted the bill for his forthcoming album. Like nearly everything from composers John Kander and Fred Ebb, whose credits included *Cabaret* and *Chicago*, 'New York, New York' sounded like a classic. By the time Sinatra got through with it, it actually became one.

A HOMECOMING OF SORTS

Fittingly, the anthem to 'the city that never sleeps' came to life in New York City itself – at the majestic old 30th Street Studio, to be exact. In 1979 it was enjoying its 30th year as a going concern. For Sinatra, the session was a homecoming of sorts. As a Columbia artist in the late 1940s, Sinatra was among the first to cut sessions at the newly opened 30th Street (his 1948 release, *The Voice of Frank Sinatra*, became the first long-playing pop record in history). But an ongoing feud with A&R man Mitch Miller led to Sinatra's departure in 1953. As a Capitol artist, who later founded his own label, Reprise, Sinatra recorded almost exclusively in California over the next 15 years.

In 1968, Sinatra returned to New York and 30th Street Studio for the making of *Cycles*, the first in a series of albums produced by Don Costa with Frank Laico engineering. "After that first session, Sinatra came up to me and handed me a roll of bills as a way of saying 'Thank you,'" remembers Laico. "I told him, 'Please, I can't accept the money. He said, 'I can appreciate that, but you do have a wife and children, right?' And I told him I did, and he said, 'And you're here most nights until midnight, so you probably don't see them that often, correct?' So he told me to give the money to my wife Colette and have her pick out the best restaurant around so we could all go out to have a nice dinner. I told him I could live with that – but just this once."

Recorded by Laico in a closed-door session on the evening of September 17th, 1979, 'Theme from New York, New York' leapt all the way up to Number 32 when released as a single the following May. It was Sinatra's first Top 40 place since 1969's 'My Way' and also his last overall.

> "LIKE NEARLY EVERYTHING KANDER & EBB WROTE, 'NEW YORK, NEW YORK' SOUNDED LIKE A CLASSIC. ONCE SINATRA GOT THROUGH WITH IT, IT BECAME ONE."

Today, Laico – who himself spent a lifetime in the city that never sleeps – proudly displays the gold record presented to him for services rendered on the wall above his home stereo system. When I interviewed him and ex-Columbia A&R man Mitch Miller recently, I wondered aloud if there was something ironic about Sinatra returning to 30th Street to record 'New York, New York.' Laico turns to Miller and says: "You didn't know, but I was recording Sinatra at that time." He pauses as Miller looks puzzled.

"I wound up doing six albums with him," Laico continues. "Don Costa called and literally begged me to do the session ... and I told him, 'You know, Don, I could get into trouble, we're not supposed to be doing other labels.' So for that *Trilogy* album, they arranged it, and Sinatra said we couldn't have any audience in the studio, otherwise we'd blow it. And one of them ended up being 'New York, New York,' which turned out to be Frank's last hit."

Miller is aghast. "He did that at 30th Street? No! I don't believe it!" I chip in to tell him that that's what I meant by ironic. "I did not know that until now!" says Miller. Not only was it Sinatra's last hit, I continue, but as it turns out, it was also the last hit produced at 30th Street. Laico says: "I don't even think it impressed Sinatra all that much. I don't believe he thought it had hit potential."

I ask Laico and Miller if it might have been Sinatra's idea to do that session at 30th Street. "Perhaps," says Laico. "He may have gone to Don and asked to cut it there, seeing as he was going to be in New York." And Miller concludes: "Well, he sure did know how he would sound in there!"

LIKE A VIRGIN

While a revitalized Frank Sinatra was riding the charts, in a small apartment in lower Manhattan, 22-year-old Madonna Ciccone, an aspiring actress/model, was assembling a resumé for the benefit of New York's PR agencies. Consisting mainly of bit parts in small promotional films, Ciccone's list also included the attribute "Drummer/Songwriter," buried near the bottom. It would take two more years for Madonna (who by then had jettisoned her family name) to discover that her musical skills could actually pay the rent – especially after signing with Seymour Stein's Sire Records and scoring a pair of nationwide dance hits in 'Lucky Star' and 'Borderline.' By the end of 1983, Madonna's self-titled debut album had gone platinum.

Nothing, however, could have prepared the public for the stunning 1984 break-out *Like a Virgin*, recorded with ace producer Nile Rodgers at the Power Station, the studio founded in 1977 by New Jersey's Tony Bongiovi (and current home to Avatar Studios).

Located well off the grid at 53rd Street near 10th Avenue, Power Station (named for its original owner, New York utility ConEdison) bucked the shrinking-studio trend of the late 1970s with a main recording room capable of holding a full orchestra and a control room featuring a 32-channel Neve 8068 console, with a full compliment of UREI limiters and a bank of 24 Pultec EQs (modified so that the Pultec's tubes could be accessed separately without any coloring, if so desired). A pair of Neumann condensers suspended high in the air helped capture the studio's ample air space (giving Bruce Springsteen's *The River* as well as David Bowie's comeback-capping *Let's Dance* their tremendous live sound).

In contrast to Madonna's tech-heavy first album, producer Rodgers envisioned a much simpler set-up, and backed the singer with an economical rhythm section consisting of bassist Bernard Edwards (Rodgers' partner in the dance group Chic), drummer Tony Thompson (whose pounding rhythms had juiced the Bowie single), with Rodgers himself handling the guitar parts.

The concept worked brilliantly. In November, 'Like a Virgin' – the album's title-track, co-written by pop tunesmith Billy Steinberg – revealed a tougher, hard-pop Madonna, a sound so irresistible that even rock radio took notice. Propelling the single was Thompson's massive snare backbeat, carefully sculpted by Rodgers' main engineer, Jason Corsaro.

"Tony's got such a great way with drums – he plays so hard and so loud he just fills the room up with sound," notes Corsaro. "I realized that it was something that had to be captured. I mean, if you've got a drummer who sounds so beautiful in the room, why would you want to take that away?"

Ever since the days of disco, dance-pop rhythm parts had maintained a relatively unobtrusive role in the mix – and initially Corsaro's attempt at defying R&B tradition was met with resistance. "Before we did *Like a Virgin*, there was a Chic record called *Believer*," says Corsaro, "and I'd been trying to do the same thing on that – open up the room sound on the drums but still keep it R&B. But the folks at Power Station were always telling me, 'You can't put R&B drums in the big room, they have to go in the dead room.' But that didn't make any sense to me – I knew there had to be a way to capture the power of the drums and keep the rhythm at the same time."

Corsaro eventually figured out a unique method that involved equal parts mic placement and just plain technical creativity. "By being too close, I knew I was going to miss a lot of those dynamics. By the same token, that music demanded a strong groove. So I started cutting the room tracks in time with the drums. Everyone thinks it was gated, but I actually wrote the parts into the computer as we were mixing. On the SSL those cut switches were very fast, so I just sat there and wrote them in, and fixed them if they got out of time. When I added Tony's drums on top of that, the sound was incredibly powerful. It was just what I wanted – a rock, room sound, but also very R&B."

Placed in the center of the minimalist mix of 'Like a Virgin,' Thompson's drum kit became the featured instrument. "That's one of the things that made it so special. Because there was only guitar and a bass around it, there was so much space for the drums to fill," says Corsaro. "You could hear what Tony was doing so clearly." Corsaro still had some selling to do during the initial playbacks. "To tell you the truth, Nile wasn't

■ **MARSHALL CRENSHAW (musician) "My favorite studio during the 1980s was the Power Station. At the time it was really the happening place to record, but they applied a lot of old-school principles there. The room was pretty monumental and beautifully designed, with lots of wood that gave it a really nice sound with a lot of character. They had racks-full of Pultec tube EQs as well. I did my second album, *Field Day*, in that studio, and it gave it that real tube-ish kind of sound, which was great for me. The atmosphere there was cool – Nile Rodgers was always around, there was a nice little beehive of activity going on in that building at the time. The stuff Niles did at Power Station was always very live-sounding. The great thing is that it hasn't lost that vibe, it's the place where everyone wants to make jazz records or vocalist records. It's hardly a dinosaur."**

that into it in the beginning of the record," recalls Corsaro. "It really went against the grain of the early-1980s dance sound. I think he's was looking for something a bit more 'normal.' But Madonna and her manager absolutely loved it. And that was all he needed to hear."

From a historical perspective, Corsaro's innovation played a major role in helping cross Madonna from a pure dance act into the rock mainstream – an almost unheard-of feat for the time.

"I was thrilled when they picked 'Like a Virgin' for the single," says Corsaro. "It became the first dance-pop record to have a real rock drum sound in a long time. Of course, since then Madonna's proved herself quite capable at keeping up with new ideas – it's really one of her better attributes."

> **"VERY FEW PEOPLE RUNNING THE RECORD BUSINESS HAD A MUSIC BACKGROUND ... AND THAT'S WHEN THEY MANDATED THAT THE 30TH STREET STUDIO BE CLOSED."**

Reaching Number One on December 22nd, 1984, the title track to *Like a Virgin* remained at the top of the charts for the first five weeks of 1985 (with the album hitting the top in early February), becoming Madonna's biggest career single. *Like a Virgin* spawned five additional smash hits in 'Material Girl,' 'Crazy for You,' 'Angel' (whose flip, 'Into the Groove,' became a million-selling R&B smash) and 'Dress You Up.' Madonna never looked back, dominating the pop charts with 10 consecutive Top Five hit singles through the remainder of the decade.

"I don't think you should base a record on a great drum sound with a song to go with it – it's got to be the other way around," notes Corsaro. "On the other hand, if it means someone's paying attention to the music because of that drum sound, that's a great thing.

DIGITAL ARRIVES

The arrival of magnetic tape near the end of the 1940s brought to an end the 25-year reign of wax-disc recording. And after a quarter century of reel-to-reel, a new medium emerged that would alter the music-making process as never before. It began with researcher Thom Stockham who, in 1976, spearheaded the push towards computer-based sound recording, a goal he achieved two years later with the introduction of the Soundstream digital multi-track recorder, which processed signals as 'sound files' to a fixed disc. Also in 1976, EMT, manufacturer of echo plates, offered its first digital reverberation unit, the Model 250. Meanwhile, integrated circuits suddenly began popping up in recording apparatus in major studios around the world. By the end of the decade, Sony joined the digital ranks with its 3324 multitrack recorder, as the Japanese assumed a leadership role they would never relinquish in digital manufacturing.

Digital recording offered a number of distinct advantages, not the least of which was the ability for engineers to edit and manipulate tracks quickly and easily, without the hassle of razor blades and splicing tape. Of equal importance, however, were the time- and space-saving benefits wrought by digitally reinforced signal processing, which made it possible to 'sample' the sound of an analog source such as a live echo chamber or tape delay for use in effects racks and pedal units.

In 1979, the majors finally succeeded in killing off disco, replaced punk with the antiseptic new wave movement, and elevated hoary rockers like Styx and REO Speedwagon to god-like status. In response, a confused record-buying public handed the industry its first major setback in three decades, sending sales plummeting more than 10 percent year-to-year. After years of rampant excess that included completely modernized recording studios outfitted with hot tubs, kitchens, and recreational facilities, record-company bosses frantically sought to cut loose all the extra baggage. At CBS alone, some 7,000 positions were eliminated during the first part of the 1980s. In a cost-cutting frenzy, nothing is sacred; in mid 1982 Columbia's management suddenly realized it had one recording facility too many and decided to pull the plug on its historic 30th Street Studio.

"At the time 30th Street went under," says Don Puluse, "classical recording techniques were still in play. It was the political stuff, plus there were a lot of maintenance issues. I was actually involved with a group of people who were interested in using the studio as a multi-media facility. But the back wall needed to be reinforced. There was a lot of work that needed to be done.

"But what really happened was the company started devaluing the studio. One of the reasons was because there was a condo adjacent to the building, and the owner of the place was politically connected, and he'd actually have his books fall off his spiral staircase just so he could complain. So this went on for some time.

"The thing is, CBS could've bought the guy's building for like $250,000, but they didn't. As a result, eventually all the sessions had to end by 10 or 11pm. There became major restrictions on the recording time. Everybody respected that place, but the restrictions became really tough to deal with. Still, I'm not sure it was a necessity. Shortly after they sold the place for $1.2million, it went back on to the market for around $4.5million! I remember Teo Macero calling the CBS offices after looking at the ad in the paper and saying, 'You see what they're asking for it now? You guys are idiots!'"

According to Frank Laico, "Because the hit records that were coming out at the time were being produced in someone's basement or garage, the record companies began rethinking the whole situation. And in a studio like mine, no matter how hard you tried, you couldn't get that dead, dry sound that you heard on those recordings. So the first year that CBS posted a loss – after all the years of running major profits – the higher-ups looked at the balance sheet and decided that if things were in the red now, then they'd be in the red for the next several years as well.

"At that time, a big part of the problem was that almost all of the people who'd been hired to run the record business didn't even have a music background. To them, it was like any kind of business. Which was a real break from the way things were in the past. So that's when they turned around and mandated that 30th Street be closed – just like that. They sold the building for $1.2million. That was it."

Over the next several years the newer, smaller technology, combined with increasing property values, began to transform the market. By the 1990s, nearly all of New York's largest studios – RCA, Mediasound, the Pythian Temple, Webster Hall and others – had ceased to exist, their equipment sold at auction and the buildings transformed into offices, apartments and nightclubs.

Laico had turned down numerous offers to work at competing studios over the course of his career, but now the end of 30th Street marked the end of his affiliation with

■ **MARSHALL CRENSHAW (musician)** "The bigger rooms started closing with the justification that there weren't big combos any more, that rock had downsized everything. But at the same time, you started losing some of the life you once had on record – for the simple reason that in a smaller room you're not hearing all the unique dynamics that occur within a large, open space. To some observers, that's the point where the industry began taking a turn. I know times change, everything's constantly in flux. The good news is that there are still a few of these kinds of places around the world. But I wish there were more of them."

■ **ARTIE BUTLER (producer-arranger)** "It really represented the changing of the guard. When you had that kind of room, you're moving air, and it makes such a difference in the sound of the recording. There were so many places like that around town back then – RCA, Webster Hall, all big, beautiful rooms with lots of space."

CBS, after nearly 40 years of service, most of them at The Church. "I left in 1982, and I really didn't want to leave, though they made it plain that they wanted me out," says Laico. "So when I got the deal I wanted, I left.

"A short time later I got a call from a friend of mine, who offered me a job as their chief engineer. I told him I was still too angry from the CBS experience, but that if I did, I'd only do it under two conditions – that I didn't have to go into New York, and that I didn't have to record to multi-track!

"Even when I was working 24-track, I still applied the two-track mentality – I'd pay attention to what was going on the tracks and set my balances as I was going along, so that if I had to go back to the original tape all I'd have to do is just bring up the levels again and that would be it. My rationale was that we'd get the job done faster, it'd be a better product, and yet it would still sound great. The musicians would be told in advance that there won't be any overdubbing, so they'd have to get it right the first time. So my friend thought about it for a bit and then got back to me and said, 'OK, that sounds good. Now where are we going to do this?' So we looked around and ended up finding a few suitable spots to make the recordings."

Not surprisingly, Laico's first choice was a house of worship: a Jewish synagogue located in nearby Rye, New York. "That worked great for the first few albums, but when it came time to do a Christmas album, the rabbi said, 'Sorry Frank, I don't think we let you do that one here,'" says Laico. "So we ended up at a chapel at a nearby college – which, of course, turned out to be yet another acoustically perfect room. And they had one of the really nice old organs in there, which really made it great, because it was Victorian Christmas music. I told the school headmaster, be prepared, because when this album comes out, I guarantee that you're going to get besieged by requests from other record companies to come in and use this place. Sure enough, within years, Columbia had been there, along with RCA, EMI and others. So I did that for the next 10 years."

At 72, Laico thought he'd mixed his last session when, in 1990, he received a phone call from an old friend, requesting his presence in the studio. "Tony [Bennett] called me up from Vegas one night," says Laico, "and asked if I would help him put together this collection that became the *Forty Years* Columbia-Legacy box.

"I went down there and listened to what they'd done so far, and it sounded OK, except Danny [Bennett's son and manager], being a rock musician, had equalized the piss out of it – he'd added all this bass to everything. So I said, 'Let's take a listen to the original track,' and it was obvious at that point. So Danny left us alone, and we went to work. It just took a day and a half, and by the time we got up to the stuff from the 1970s, there wasn't much changing at all." With Tony Bennett on the comeback trail, in 1991 Laico found himself back in the studio with his favorite artist for the making of *Perfectly Frank*, a Sinatra tribute album.

More than 40 years had passed since Laico's first session with Bennett at 30th Street Studio, making theirs the longest surviving artist-engineer relationship in history. "And then that was it for me," says Laico, who finally called it a day after a half-century of service. "I can't say that I really miss it, though it's not like I haven't thought about being back in the studio from time to time. But can you imagine some guy walking in and setting up the room with hearing aids in each ear? That would be pretty funny."

EPILOGUE

"When we were doing four and eight-track, I could listen to a record that was made in New York and tell you which studio it came from," says engineer Shelly Yakus. "When we went to 16-track, it was tougher, and when we went to 24 I couldn't tell any more. The studios in New York all had distinctive sounds, a combination of the rooms, the equipment, and the main engineers who were doing them.

"I learned the sound of Bell, of A&R, of Mediasound, of Mira Sound," Yakus continues. "You could hear it on the radio.

"But it all went out the window with 24-track. 16 tracks on two-inch tape was as far as you could go and still maintain the personality of a room. The 24-track machines started to eat up the clarity of the instruments."

"The way it used to be was that everyone would have to get together and play together – and there's something completely unique when that happens," notes Chris Huston. "That's why those old records sound so good! It's not rocket science. The reason why these 'oldies' compare favorably to their technologically superior counterparts is because you're hearing the magic in the room at that session.

"You know that something exceptional was going on in that room if it's a great record. There's no doubt about it! You hear the drums bouncing off the walls, all these different

■ MARSHALL CRENSHAW (musician) "Very often I can listen to a song and be able to tell which studio it was recorded at, or know which region it came from. But I can't do that at all now. Which isn't to say that all records made today sound generic. But as far as listening to a record and getting a specific sense of place, I don't really hear that right any more – I think it's gone."

sounds moving and blending together, all these things are happening that you wouldn't put up with in a studio nowadays."

"Back then, in order to make a record, you had to put people in a room," says Marshall Crenshaw. "Of course, that's all changed, now you just have to put something right in front of a microphone, or, for that matter, just plug it straight in, to the point that the room element is unnecessary. I love that sense of collective energy that you get when listening to old records, this cooperative spirit that comes right through."

The question remains: are we really better off today as a result of the inevitable progression of technology? "I always tell people, 'If the music's right, you don't hear the hiss,'" says Huston. "When that happens, all of the technical things that are 'wrong' fall by the wayside. And many times, they actually support the music."

"You hear George Martin talk about this – would the Beatles have done as well in today's recording environment?" says Don Puluse. "Where would they have been without having the performance aspect that was so much a part of their early years? The fact that you don't have to rewind tape any more – is that a good or bad thing? Some people say it's great, your mind is constantly on the move, therefore you get to keep the creative process flowing. Other people say, 'No, those extra few minutes that you had while the engineer was spooling back was refreshing, it was a necessary part of the studio process.' I can see both sides. It's great to have a real grasp on classical techniques and be able to apply that to today's machinery. One thing's for sure. As the technology changes, the essence of the musician changes along with it."

In 2004, studio owners in New York and elsewhere face an industry in a perpetual state of consolidation, recording music that has little need for old-fashioned acoustics. New York native Lou Gonzalez – one of the few veteran engineers still in town – gives voice to the uncertainty that marks the Manhattan of the 21st century.

"Things are tough here now," says Gonzalez. "The thing is, recording in New York used to be fun. Unfortunately, it's really not that much fun any more. You picked a good time to put out this book – another year, and there might not be anything left here at all."

new york grooves

Elvis records 'Hound Dog' with The Jordanaires, bassist Bill Black, drummer DJ Fontana, and guitarist Scotty Moore, RCA 'A', July 1956.

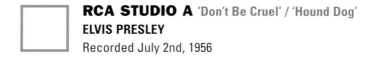

RCA STUDIO A 'Don't Be Cruel' / 'Hound Dog'
ELVIS PRESLEY
Recorded July 2nd, 1956

"Elvis used to listen to our radio shows on the Grand Ole Opry," recalls Jordanaires vocalist Gordon Stoker, "and he loved our sound, because it was the same kind of gospel-influenced singing he'd heard while growing up. He knew right then that if he landed a major recording contract, he wanted us on his records."

When Presley secured a deal with RCA a few months later, Stoker got the call. 'I Was the One' and 'I Want You, I Need You, I Love You' featured Stoker alongside Speer Family singers Ben and Brock Speer, but for his next effort, Presley insisted on the real deal. On July 2nd, 1956, all four Jordanaires met Presley inside RCA's massive Studio A and cut the double-sided smash 'Don't Be Cruel' / 'Hound Dog.' It was the start of a musical relationship that would last 14 years.

Located at 155 East 24th Street near Lexington Avenue, RCA's Studio A was an architectural marvel, a huge room with immense walls and ceilings, originally designed for jazz orchestras (including those of Glen Miller, Duke Ellington, and many others). Portions of the walls and ceilings could even be moved in or out at will in order to shape the acoustics during a session.

Presley's on-mic manner presented engineers with an unusual challenge. The original king of bump'n'grind on stage, Presley was no less stable inside a recording studio. Rather than cramp his style, RCA's technical staff simply surrounded Presley with three different microphones (including RCA 44BX and 77DX ribbon mics), thereby ensuring error-free vocal transmission.

"What made Elvis unique was his insistence that we be given credit on the recordings," notes Stoker. "Back then – and for years after – studio musicians were seldom credited, even though they frequently came up with the arrangements, the tempo, added licks and such. Elvis was different – probably because of the way he'd come up in the business – and he went to great lengths to make sure we were given our due."

When Presley manager Colonel Tom Parker began pulling the singer away from his rock'n'roll roots, New Yorkers Jerry Leiber and Mike Stoller attempted to intervene. "It was Leiber and Stoller who once said that in Elvis the Colonel knew he had the golden goose," says historian Matt Goldman. "And he wanted the goose to keep putting out the same golden eggs all the time. So when Leiber and Stoller came to Elvis and said, 'You know, you have this exceptional talent and we can get you into some really great, challenging situations,' the Colonel stepped in and said, 'You stay away from my boy, understand?' And that basically became the way Elvis's career played out, right until the end."

Dozens of lame movies (and dozens more jelly donuts) can never obscure the vitality of those initial RCA tracks. **"**I remember we were doing a Marshall Crenshaw track once down at RCA," recalls producer Ed Stasium. "They'd put in some new equipment there, and the stuff kept breaking down, and I was going crazy. So to appease us, they let us go down into the basement where the vault was, because they knew we'd find some interesting stuff down there.

"And sure enough, there's these Glenn Miller acetates, things like that ... and then we found these tape boxes marked 'ELVIS.' It's me, Marshall and Paul Shaffer, who was there playing keyboards, and our mouths just dropped open! So we go running upstairs with the tapes, and it's the sessions for 'His Latest Flame' and 'Little Sister.' It's just a running tape about 20 minutes long, and there's a splice where they cut out the master take. And it's beautiful – you hear the mix changing as it goes along, they're fixing the instrumentation, adding different bass parts, putting in bongos, then taking them out, the banter in between.

"But most of all, the sound of that one tape was just *amazing* – it was so alive! But it's something you can't really re-capture, because it was about that particular studio, that time, the players, everything. Which is why every time I hear those sessions, I'm thinking to myself, 'How come I can't get *my* records to sound like *this*?'"

WORLD UNITED STUDIOS 'Walk Away Renee'
LEFT BANKE
Recorded June 15th, 1966

Violinist Harry Lookofsky was a unique talent – a Kentucky-born, New York transplant whose 1958 release *Stringsville* is widely regarded as the first bebop jazz violin recording ever made. For three decades, Lookofksy was one of the city's most in-demand session string players. "He came to be known as the guy who could handle the tricky rhythms and the complicated riffs right off," remarked his wife Sherry Lookofsky. "He practised all the time so he would be ready. Because if you didn't sound good, you didn't get hired the next time."

In the mid-1960s, Lookofsky opened his own micro-facility, dubbed World United Studios, located near the Brill Building at 1595 Broadway. Assisting him was his teenaged son Michael – aka Michael Brown – who eventually began cutting tracks with a group of friends under the name Left Banke. Brown was also an occasional songwriter, who found his muse one day in 1966 when bassist Tom Finn arrived with a blonde 16-year-old female companion named Renee Fladen.

An infatuated Brown dashed off a set of love-struck ballads, including the painfully obvious 'Walk Away Renee.' The band cut the track live behind vocalist Steve Martin, though Brown later admitted that his harpsichord part was overdubbed. "My hands were shaking when I tried to play, because she was right there in the control room," he recalled. "There was no way I could do it with her around, so I came back and did it later."

The elder Lookofsky handled all the string parts, then began shopping the track around town. His persistence paid off when Smash Records released 'Walk Away Renee' as a single in the fall of 1966. It made it all the way up to Number Five and was followed by another Brown-composed paean to Fladen, 'Pretty Ballerina.' In the 1970s Brown formed the band Stories ('Brother Louie'), while Lookofsky maintained a packed session schedule in addition to operating Sound Ideas Studios with partner George Klabin. Lookofsky passed away in 1998.

"Harry was always very disciplined," says Sherry Lookofsky. "Like when he was trying to get his son's band heard: he must have called every record company there was, but everyone was always 'in a meeting.' When 'Walk Away Renee' hit, suddenly they were all calling Harry – but he just told them that *he* was in a meeting!"

ALLEGRO RECORDING STUDIO 'Mony Mony'
TOMMY JAMES AND THE SHONDELLS
Recorded January 1968

"The night we wrote the song, we were absolutely devastated because we couldn't come up with a 'Bony Moronie,' a 'Sloopy' kind of title, and we knew that's what it had to be," recalls Tommy James.

"It had to be a girl's name that nobody had ever heard of before. We were going through the dictionary, but nothing was happening. We were just absolutely frustrated. I walked out onto my terrace – I lived in Manhattan at the time – and I'm just sort of scanning around and I'm looking for just any part of a name, anything."

At that moment, James was struck by the sight of a flashing neon sign atop the 40-story Mutual Of New York insurance building, located right up the street at 1740

Broadway. "I said [to my manager], 'Ritchie, c'mere.' He came over and I said, 'Look.' And all of a sudden, here's this 'M.O.N.Y' with a dollar sign in the middle of the O. The song kind of etched in stone in New York, I guess. We both just fell down laughing."

Like most of the Shondells hits since 1966, 'Mony Mony' came to life at Allegro Recording Studio at 1650 Broadway, located in the basement of the same building that housed Don Kirshner's Aldon Music and Florence Greenberg's original Scepter Records studio. Owned by Charlie Brave, Allegro was a modest four-track studio with a dry tracking room but a superb live chamber (best heard on The 4 Seasons' 1964 smash 'Rag Doll'). "Allegro was a hot studio in the 1960s," recalls engineer Rod McBrien, who cut tracks for Mitch Ryder & The Detroit Wheels, The Critters and Bobby Bloom, in addition to The Shondells. "Being in the basement, you could actually hear the 1 & 9 subway, which ran right underneath Broadway. Of course the music covered it up, but you wouldn't want to do a spoken-word record in there!"

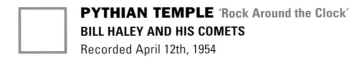

PYTHIAN TEMPLE 'Rock Around the Clock'
BILL HALEY AND HIS COMETS
Recorded April 12th, 1954

As it turns out, some of the best rooms in Manhattan had been designed not for recording, but for praying. One such place was the Pythian Temple, located uptown at 135 West 70th Street and home to the Decca label and its subsidiary, Coral. Designed in the 1920s by architect Thomas Lamb, the Pythian once served as a meeting facility for the lodges of the Knights of Pythias, and featured a quartet of ten-foot-tall pharaohs who greeted visitors who entered through the temple's main gates.

On the third floor sat an immense auditorium, with high ceilings, balconies adorned with hanging drapes, and a wide, open wooden floor. In the early 1940s Decca transformed the palatial room into a recording studio, and over the next 15 years welcomed artists ranging from Billie Holiday, Coleman Hawkins and Louis Jordan to early rockers like Johnny Burnette and Buddy Holly.

One of the key players at Decca was Milt Gabler, a visionary record producer with a penchant for exploring uncharted territory. In 1939, Gabler's Commodore label issued Billie Holiday's 'Strange Fruit,' a controversial song about Southern lynching, after Holiday's own label, Columbia, refused to release the record. Some 15 years later, Gabler would once again test the parameters of the music industry from the floor of the Pythian. The date was April 12th, 1954; the group was Bill Haley and his Comets. The song: 'Rock Around the Clock.' "At the Pythian, you could blow, because there was this big high ceiling. We had drapes hanging from the balconies, and a live wooden floor," remembered Gabler, who instructed the engineers to open up the pots in order to capture the hot sounds rising from Pythian's recording floor.

"When they got it down … that thing rocked! I had three mics on the drums alone. We had the guy slap the bass … then I had the steel player hit what I called lightning flashes, where he'd take the steel bar and hit it across the strings of the steel guitar and make it arc."

With its inclusion in the 1955 film *Blackboard Jungle*, 'Rock Around the Clock' became an instant smash, single-handedly touching off the rock'n'roll explosion, no doubt aided by the Pythian's explosive sound. Some 50 years on, the record has sold over 25million copies.

FINE SOUND STUDIOS 'Daydream'
ELLA FITZGERALD & THE DUKE ELLINGTON ORCHESTRA
Recorded June 24th, 1957

This four minute masterpiece came together inside a converted record factory located across the river in Bayside, Queens. It was one of three facilities owned by renowned engineer C. Robert Fine, a master of simplicity who often cut entire symphony orchestras using a single U47 microphone.

"Though the Bayside room was quite big – more so than RCA's studios, in fact – it wasn't very reverberant," recalls producer/engineer Elliot Mazer. "It sounded tight and smooth, and would have a been a great room for rock bands. We cut Clark Terry, Maynard Ferguson, and Teddy Wilson records there."

But the finest of them all was Fine Sound Studio A, built out of the main ballroom of the Great Northern Hotel on West 57th Street near 6th Avenue (the current site of Le Parker Meridian Hotel), complete with such original features as stately chandeliers, hand-sculpted columns, and illuminated stained-glass ceilings.

"The room had almost no acoustical treatment – it naturally had a nice, round sound," says Walter Sear, a Fine disciple who later launched the first of several Sear Sound studios from the 57th St. location. "You had to walk through the studio to get to the control room, the bathrooms were the public hotel restrooms across the hall, and the columns somewhat restricted the view, but it didn't matter – it was a beautiful place, a grand old lady of its time."

JUGGY SOUND STUDIO 'Ramble On'
LED ZEPPELIN
Recorded June 1969

During a 1968 meeting with future Led Zeppelin vocalist Robert Plant, guitarist Jimmy Page described his idea for a band that could combine the intensity of hard rock with "a lot of light and shade." 'Dazed And Confused' and the acoustic-electric 'Babe I'm Gonna Leave You' – both from Led Zeppelin's self-titled debut – proved that the 24-year-old Page, an accomplished session man with studio skills beyond his years, was on the right track. With the band's second effort, released late in 1969, Page scored a direct hit.

Today, the dynamic elements and studio artistry that combined to make *Led Zeppelin II* a cornerstone of hard rock are no less powerful. Ironically, many of the songs on the album – 'Whole Lotta Love,' 'Ramble On,' 'Heartbreaker' – were assembled piece by piece at a half-dozen stateside demo studios while the band was in the midst of a gruelling 1969 tour. One such facility was Juggy Sound Studio on West 54th Street, where the band recorded 'Ramble On' and portions of 'What Is And What Should Never Be' in early June. Though it was only a modest eight-track facility, Page used every inch of Juggy's available space to good advantage. "Instead of just going right up against the grille," Page once observed, "I'd put mics in the back of the amps, and way out in the room as well – you can really hear that at the end of 'What Is and What Should Never Be.' The point is, if you can get the sound of the room in there, you're bound to capture the emotion of the recording – much more so than if everything's going direct."

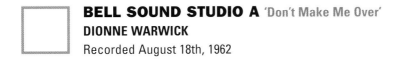

BELL SOUND STUDIO A 'Don't Make Me Over'
DIONNE WARWICK
Recorded August 18th, 1962

Florence Greenberg's early success with the Goffin-King penned 'Will You Love Me Tomorrow' created a new outlet for the writers who frequented the Scepter offices at 1650 Broadway. After a re-release of 1959's 'Dedicated to the One I Love' and 'Mama Said' returned the Shirelles to the Top Ten, Greenberg spent the next six months looking for the group's next big smash. In early 1962, she finally got one in 'Baby It's You,' which eventually reached Number Eight. The song came courtesy of veteran Tin Pan Alley songsmith Bob Hilliard, and his 32-year-old partner Burt Bacharach, a composer/producer/arranger who'd achieved moderate success with the likes of Marty Robbins and Connie Stevens during the 1950s.

With lyricist Hal David, Bacharach began a string of impeccably crafted hit singles, the majority of which were produced at Bell Sound and centered on the vocal talent of a former demo singer from Newark by the name of Dionne Warwick, whom Bacharach had encountered during a demo session for another Hilliard-Bacharach tune, 'Mexican Divorce.'

"I was introduced to Dionne and her cousin Cissy Huston when they came in to do the backgrounds on my demos," remarks engineer Brooks Arthur. "They were getting $25 a piece, $30 if we double-tracked!

Around this time Burt was looking for a singer, and I told him about Dionne. Burt was doing a demo on a song called 'Don't Make Me Over' at Associated. Dionne did that, after which they went over to Bell to do the master – and the rest is history."

Recorded on August 18th, 1962 at Bell's Studio A, Warwick's rendition of 'Don't Make Me Over' eventually found its way to Number 21 on the Hot 100.

Over the next ten years, she would score an additional 30 Top 40 hits while signed to Scepter. Entries like 'Walk on By,' 'Here I Am' and 'The Windows of the World' bear the unmistakable stamp of its producer: a supple rhythm track featuring piano, horns and the characteristic electric-guitar 'chinks,' with a supple string section fleshing out the proceedings.

"Gary Chester was a major part of the sound of those Bacharach records," says Artie Butler. "It's that quasi bossa-nova feel that you hear on the drums. Gary had a way of playing that 'loop,' as we used to call it. He did it using a brush stroke that came up on the up-beat, it was incredibly different and really gave those productions that unique flavor.

"The thing about the big studios is that, despite their greatness, a lot of times they wouldn't have a tight rhythm-section sound with a live orchestra," says Butler.

"But the Bacharach records at Bell were always a lot tighter – mainly because of engineer Eddie Smith, who would actually put a little U-shaped separator in front of the drums. Eddie Smith was a blues guy who was also an arranger, so he understood rhythm sections. He'd mixed a lot of the sessions for King: James Brown and such. He was an absolutely fabulous engineer."

WEBSTER HALL 'Banana Boat (Day-O)'
HARRY BELAFONTE
Recorded October 20th, 1955

Backed by bassist Milt Hinton and percussionist Osie Johnson, "The Banana Boat Song" became the highlight of Harlem-born Harry Belafonte's third RCA release, 1956's *Calypso*, which launched the infamous 1950s dance craze and became the first LP by a solo artist (and a black solo artist, no less) to sell over a million copies.

Calypso was one of the many notable albums conceived at RCA's Webster Hall studios, located at 125 11th Street in New York's East Village. Constructed in the late 1800s, the beautifully appointed hall served as a popular meeting spot for both social and political events throughout the early 20th century. In an effort to keep pace with Columbia's bustling studio system, in the early 1950s RCA converted the hall into a full-service recording studio, which served as a companion to the label's main studios on East 24th Street. A popular venue for Broadway-cast and pop-vocal albums, the Webster also turned out scores of jazz classics, including the great *Jazz Samba Encore!* featuring sax man Stan Getz with guitarists Antonio Carlos Jobim and Luis Bonfa.

"At Webster Hall, they had a large theatre curtain that they'd move into place in order to control the amount of room reverb," says producer Creed Taylor. "RCA had the place Monday through Friday for recording sessions. Then they put up a glass booth on the side of this immense dance hall so they could rent the space out on weekends."

"It was a cavernous, hockey rink of a studio," recalled Joel Dorn, producer of Roland Kirk's 1967 effort *The Inflated Tear*, "the same place where Eddie Fisher made 'Dungaree Doll' and Sergeant Barry Sadler gave us 'The Ballad Of The Green Berets.' The walls were elementary-school-boys'-room gray, and the engineers were union guys who wore ties and, to me at least, spent the bulk of their time waiting for their next break or figuring out what their pensions were going to come to each month. I did not want to make the album there. Boy, was I wrong! Acoustically, the room was perfect for that quartet. And the engineer, Paul Goodman, who went on to win a Grammy for his work with the Philadelphia Orchestra, not only captured the Zen of Rahsaan and his music, but also in particular that of this quartet."

At Columbia's 30th Street Studio, floor polishing was strictly prohibited for fear of disturbing the acoustic balance. Not so at Webster Hall, says producer Elliot Mazer. "During one session, the engineers suddenly got up and told us that we had to take a break because they waxed the studio floors every Wednesday evening," says Mazer. "I couldn't believe it, but sure enough at 8pm sharp, they broke down the entire studio for the wax job, then had to set it all up again maybe 45 minutes later."

CENTURY SOUND STUDIO 'Sweet Caroline'
NEIL DIAMOND
Recorded February 1969

Two years had passed since Neil Diamond's last trip to the Top Ten, but with 'Sweet Caroline,' the drought came to an end. Diamond's first smash on the Uni label was polished off by longtime producer engineer Brooks Arthur at Arthur's own Century Sound Studio, a former broadcast studio located at 135 West 52nd Street. "The studio was a flight up with no elevator," recalls Arthur, "with a recording room about 25 by 50 feet, with a small control room. It had an Electrodyne board, the first one, and Scully two, four and eight-track machines. I had an EMT chamber that I kept upstairs in an isolation room, and I also had a Fisher spring box as well. Also I had two Fairchild compressors, LA2A, Urei compressors, Altec 604s for monitors, and KLHs as well, along with the usual complement of mics."

Shortly after opening Century in 1967, Arthur played host to an unusual group of Californians calling themselves The Grateful Dead, then working on their second album for Warners. "Talk about culture shock," laughs Arthur. "These young mothers were breastfeeding in the control room while this very trippy Dead music was going down. It was the hippie culture first-hand. What an experience!"

MIRA SOUND 'Society's Child'
JANIS IAN
Recorded March 1965

The mid-1960s folk-rock scene spawned a fresh crop of politically minded songsmiths who'd grown up listening to Theodore Bikel and Odetta but came of age in the era of the Beatles and Dylan. One of those newcomers was New Jersey native Janis Ian, who proceeded to deliver one of the most controversial songs of her time.

In 1965, Ian – 14 years old at the time – entered Mira Sound on West 47th, armed with a rented 12-string and backed by a rhythm section featuring drummer Buddy Salzman and keyboarist Artie Butler. There she cut 'Society's Child,' a teen's-eye view of the hypocrisy surrounding an interracial romance. Produced by Shangri-Las' soundman

George 'Shadow' Morton, 'Society's Child' was shunned by more than 20 labels before Verve Forecast took a chance in late 1966. The single languished for several more months until Leonard Bernstein featured its singer on the now-legendary 1967 CBS TV special *Inside Pop*.

"Atlantic Records had paid for the session, but then gave me back the record and said they couldn't put it out," recalls Ian. "When it finally hit, all the people who'd turned it down were suddenly talking about what an important record it was. Still, the only apology I ever got was from Atlantic's own Jerry Wexler, who told me that he of all people should have put that record out in the first place."

Even as it was climbing the charts, 'Society's Child' touched off a firestorm of derision from both sides of the political fence. "It was a very strange time," says Ian. "On the one hand there were the people who hated it because it was about a black-white relationship. But then there were the folk people who criticized the song because it had drums on it! Which was really stupid. The point was to get the largest number of people to become aware of the problem and maybe change their minds. Being 15, you completely ignore it and act like it doesn't bother you. But of course, it did."

"I heard the song for the first time at that session," says Butler, who played both harpsichord and organ during the take. "I must've put on ten miles during that gig! Plus I was wearing headphones, so I had to be careful not to trip or make noise as I was scurrying back and forth. At the end of the record, George says to me, 'I need something right here to finish it.' And so I just came up with organ thing. I remember just hearing that organ all the time over the radio! I remember that session so vividly. I realized that we were in the presence of this really sophisticated, gifted and sensitive artist. I came up with the organ lines and the harpsichord bits, but I can't take any credit for the sound of the record, which was all Janis and George.

"Janis was like 14 going on 30," says Butler. "At that session I knew right way that this wasn't just some young kid coming in to make a one-shot record; she was a major player with something to say. The message of that song was way ahead of its time."

SUNDRAGON STUDIOS 'Psycho Killer'
TALKING HEADS
Recorded April 1977

Formed by drummer Chris Frantz, bassist Tina Weymouth and guitarist/songwriter David Byrne while students at the Rhode Island School of Design, Talking Heads possessed the quirkiness that was required of any member of lower Manhattan's CBGB society. But with the Bowery already conquered, by late 1976 Talking Heads began thinking in terms of mainstream acceptance. After shopping a few demo tapes, the band inked a deal with Seymour Stein's Sire label, and added a fourth member, ex-Modern Lover Jerry Harrison. The following April, the band began work on their debut album at Sundragon Studios, a small project facility located just off 20th Street in lower Manhattan.

"Sundragon was this very small, very dead studio," says *Talking Heads: 77* producer/engineer Ed Stasium, who'd just finished work on the Ramones' second effort *Leave Home*, also cut at Sundragon. "There was a lot of carpeting in there, the control room couldn't fit more than two or three people at a time. The recording room wasn't much bigger, about the size of a small living room. But we managed to have fun working in there.

"Compared to the Ramones, working with Talking Heads was a very different experience," says Stasium. "Whereas the Ramones had the punk attitude, just total straight-ahead loud and fast with everything on ten, the Talking Heads were college types – very thoughtful, very methodical."

Like their punk compatriots, Talking Heads worked diligently in the studio, laying down rhythm tracks live using only a few amp baffles for separation, with David Byrne singing guide lead and overdubbing final vocals later on. Stasium's mic placement and mixing skill ensured that Chris Frantz's R&B-based rhythms – key to the band's sound – would be properly presented on record.

"The drum miking was similar to the way I'd done Tommy Ramone's kit at the time," notes Stasium, "tight-miked, with a 57 for the snare, 421s for the toms, a D-12 and 421 on the kick, and either 87s or 414s for overheads. I was still miking the hi-hat at the time – that got a 451 as well."

Though Sundragon had a full compliment of signal gadgetry (including a 1960s-era gold-foil EMT plate reverb), the sound of *Talking Heads: 77* was, for the most part, bare-bones, dry and intimate – a quality that helped make 'Psycho Killer,' *77's* most notable cut (and the group's first chart entry), one of the scariest tunes ever to grace rock radio. "That was the first song that I ever finished," remarked Byrne years later. "It was a way to see if I could actually do it. And we all worked together on it."

THE RECORD PLANT 'School's Out'
ALICE COOPER
Recorded March 1972

To parents who'd long suspected that rock'n'roll was the devil's music, Alice Cooper was proof positive. In 1972, the original Man in Black Leather (born Vince Furnier in Detroit) descended on the marketplace with 'School's Out,' a chilling, feedback-laced pop opus that became Cooper's passport into millions of unsuspecting suburban homes.

Ironically, Cooper was anything but scary from the vantage point of a car-radio speaker. Early arrivals like 'I'm Eighteen,' 'Under My Wheels' and 'Be My Lover' were tuneful and catchy; by the time of 'School's Out' and its follow-up 'Elected,' Cooper and original guitarists Michael Bruce and Glen Buxton had blossomed into top-shelf writers who wove tricky chord changes and intelligent guitar and bass hooks into the songs. No less an observer than Bob Dylan referred to Alice as an "overlooked" songwriter.

"When we first started, not only did we have to compete with Zeppelin, Bowie and Black Sabbath on FM, but there was also Top 40 from the Beatles, Stones, Supremes and all the others," explains Cooper. "We had to come up with a song like 'No More Mr. Nice Guy' which would appeal to all ages. You had to have good stuff, or that was it."

Produced by Bob Ezrin with engineers Roy Cicala and Shelly Yakus, 'School's Out' took shape inside Studio A of the Record Plant at 321 West 44th Street, opened in 1968 by Gary Kellgren and Chris Stone (and now operating under the name Streetlight Studios). The building that was once home to Warner Brothers Pictures (a former screening room became the studio's main recording space, in fact) also included a main-floor Studio B, with another facility, Studio C, located ten flights up.

On a somber note, it was inside Studio A that John Lennon previewed the post-*Double Fantasy* track 'Walking on Thin Ice' just minutes before he was gunned down on the evening of December 8th, 1980.

THE HIT FACTORY 'Sir Duke'
STEVIE WONDER
Recorded January 1976

"I was offered a job at Vanguard and the Hit Factory at the same time," recalls veteran engineer Lou Gonzalez, now owner of Quad Studios in New York and Nashville. "Vanguard was paying twice as much money as the Hit Factory. But something told me to go with the Hit Factory. Mostly because of the music, and the stature I'd have there. And Ragovoy."

Gonzalez is referring to Hit Factory owner Jerry Ragovoy, noted R&B producer and co-writer of the Irma Franklin/Janis Joplin smash 'Piece of My Heart,' among others. "I helped build Jerry's second studio over on 48th Street," says Gonzalez. "But that first room was something else. BB King, the Band, the Rolling Stones all came through there. It literally was a hit factory – just one after another. Jerry had a 16-track Ampex MM1000 and a 10-channel rotary fader console, which was the last one I ever saw. His live chamber was a stairway – there was a duplex apartment and Ragovoy had one floor, and the stairway wasn't being used, so that's what he used for echo."

"That first Hit Factory on Broadway was great," recalls Elliot Mazer, who recorded several projects shortly after the facility opened in 1968. "It was a small room with a custom board. I later worked at the 48th Street room with Linda Ronstadt and Jake Holmes. The control room was comfortable and it sounded nice."

After a three-year stint as a partner in the Record Plant operations, in March 1975 Eddie Germano, a former RCA staff producer, bought the Hit Factory from Ragovoy. One of Germano's first major clients was Stevie Wonder, whose 'Sir Duke' (a commanding tribute to mentor Duke Ellington) became part of Wonder's tour de force double-set *Songs in the Key of Life*, issued in the spring of 1976.

Germano died in 2002; his son, Troy, operates several Hit Factory rooms out of the main headquarters at 421 West 54th Street. Sear Sound, New York's oldest independent studio operated by Walter Sear, currently occupies the site of Ragovoy's second facility at 353 West 48th Street.

the
out-of-towners

SIGMA SOUND STUDIO
PHILADELPHIA

By the early 1960s the city of Philadelphia, 100 miles to the south of New York, had become one of the most vibrant music spots on the map, due in large part to the popularity of *American Bandstand*, the weekly television show that featured hot new talent performing before a live audience of teenaged dancers. But when host Dick Clark moved the show west to Los Angeles in early 1964, Philly's connection to the pop world went right along with it.

In the spring of 1965, 17-year-old Philly native Barbara Mason, a singer and songwriter signed to Jimmy Bishop's Arctic label, recorded 'Yes, I'm Ready' at Virtue Studios, located on North Broad Street across from Temple University. "It almost never happened," remembers producer Weldon McDougal, who co-wrote the song. "She had a tantrum, sang it once, and stormed out. Luckily, one take was all it took."

With its silky strings and smooth backing vocals, 'Yes, I'm Ready,' which hit the Top Five that summer, became the blueprint for a new generation of Philly songwriters. Beginning in 1968, much of the magic emanated from the recording room at Sigma Sound, a simple three-story structure located at the corner of North 12th and Race Street adjacent to the Philadelphia Convention Center. At Sigma, producer Thom Bell recorded the Delfonics' romance classics 'Didn't I (Blow Your Mind This Time)' and 'La-La - Means I Love You,' before teaming with producers Kenny Gamble and Leon Huff – two of the greatest musical minds of the century – for a string of massive R&B hits that included Harold Melvin and the Blue Notes' 'If You Don't Know Me By Now,' The O'Jays' 'For the Love of Money' and many more.

Though the sound of Sigma was, with a few notable exceptions, black and urban, the studio's personnel were a cross-section of Philly's black, white, Jewish, and Italian populations. Its leader was Joe Tarsia, a monumental figure in Philadelphia music history, who got his foothold in the business purely by accident. While working as a television and radio repairman for the Philco Corporation during the late 1950s, Tarsia was asked to fix a tape recorder at a local studio. "I went down to do the job," says Tarsia, "and never left."

His timing couldn't have been better. "Dick Clark had just launched *American Bandstand* from Philadelphia," notes Tarsia, "which created a huge window of opportunity for the regional music scene." Suddenly, locals like Chubby Chucker, the Orlons, and the Dovells were going global with hits recorded at the tiny studios that laced Philly's downtown area. One such facility was Rec-O-Art – the future site of Sigma

Sound – where Tarsia began honing his engineering skills. "Rec-O-Art was run by Emil Corson, who was one of the best engineers around," recalls Tarsia.

"Corson was incredibly meticulous; everything always had to be just so. If you even touched a microphone he'd throw you out! The control room was puny, the recording room wasn't much bigger. He had a pair of Ampex 300s attached to a console with rotary faders. He simply refused to go beyond mono. Eventually he just pulled up stakes, ran off with his secretary and that was that! But, boy, did he make that place work. Go put on the Dovells' 'You Can't Sit Down'. I mean, what a sound."

Tarsia eventually took on a permanent engineering slot at the South Broad Street home of Cameo-Parkway, one of the hottest R&B factories of the time. "Still, I was giving up the financial security of my Philco job – and no one in my family was too keen on that," says Tarsia. "Especially after Dick Clark left, and that window closed right up. But then along came Kenny and Leon – and another fire got started."

Almost immediately, the Tarsia-Gamble-Huff team clicked with the Soul Survivors' fall 1967 smash 'Expressway to Your Heart.' When Cameo was purchased by music mogul Allen Klein that same year, Tarsia decided to strike out on his own. In 1968, he occupied the second floor of the former Rec-O-Art building and began making preparations for his new facility. "I wanted a real identifiable name, something like Gold Star, which I loved," says Tarsia. "One day I was sitting in a Greek restaurant, and there was a placemat with the Greek alphabet on it. And there it was."

From the outside, Sigma's brick facade suggested old-world charm; but when it came to recording technology, Sigma, like many of New York's independents, stayed well ahead of the pack. "When I first opened the place, I altered the back of the control room to make room for a Scully eight-track and four-track," says Tarsia. "I hooked them up to a big wide Electrodyne console, with Altec 604s for playback. From the edge of the console to the window was about four feet, from the other side of the room to the tape recorder was another four feet – the whole thing was like 12 x 16, tops.

"Later we had three different automated outboard systems that would allow you to mute, group, and do rides. From 1968 to 1978, Sigma led the pack in technology – I would venture to say that we were the first studio in the world to have a successful automation system. You look at the actual building, and you'd never guess – the rooms were small, there's an air conditioner hanging out the window – but when it came to equipment, we were always trying to push the envelope."

During the 1960s, the studios of Detroit, Memphis and Muscle Shoals helped define the sound of black America, but Sigma was the first studio to make that sound huge. Not that it took a ton of real estate: Tarsia built his tracks in a recording room that was barely

40 feet long by 20 feet wide. "And we had a lot of musicians in there – upwards of 30 per session," recalls the engineer.

"As a result, the instruments were always talking into each other's microphones. But I loved that – because you'd always get something unexpected. Years ago when I was learning how to make records, whenever a local producer was heading up to New York, I'd ask if I could tag along. And I'd sit in the control room and just watch how things were done, and hopefully pick up a thing or two. I remember being at Bell Sound for a Peggy March session – it was horns, vocals, strings, and everything was going at the same time. At first the drum sound was the same stinking sound I'd been getting. All of a sudden the engineer flipped open the strings mic, and suddenly, wham!, there it was – and it was just huge sounding. That left a big impression.

"One of my favorite Sigma sessions was for 'Didn't I (Blow Your Mind This Time),'" says Tarsia. "As usual, we were recording the backing track live, and we had the drums miked up a certain way. But the second we opened up the strings microphones, the whole character of the drum sound changed. Thom Bell wasn't so sure, but I knew it would be great. So I started doing stuff like that on purpose. Sometimes during the mixing process, I'd set up a pair of mics in the studio, then turn on the studio monitors and feed the track into the studio and weave some of that back into the mix. Or just hang a couple extra mics way back in the room during a strings session, just to try to get some of the room ambience and make it sound like it was a real live date."

For extra dimension, Tarsia made the most of Sigma's 40-foot long, six-foot wide echo chamber, parked directly outside ("a really sweet room"), to go with several echo plates. "Originally I had the EMTs in the back hallway," says Tarsia, "until I made a deal with the building owner to take over the basement, and eventually put the plates right down there, built up on cinder blocks and enclosed to control the environment a little bit better.

"I always loved the old CBS recordings, because they were one of the first to use a tape recorder in front of an echo chamber," says Tarsia. "And that became standard operating procedure at Sigma – we always had a machine running at 15 ips in front of our EMT. It sounded fantastic on those strings – listen to 'Me and Mrs. Jones' or 'Back Stabbers' – but you don't want a delay on everything, so I'd have a direct feed set up as well that I could switch to when necessary. Also, my hearing always lacked for high end – which meant I'd accentuate the upper frequencies, especially on the echo EQ. It's really what gave those records that identifiable sound."

In 1976 Sigma expanded its operations to include a New York facility at 1697 Broadway, all the while catering to an increasingly diverse client roster, from rockers like

Todd Rundgren (himself a Philadelphia native) to alt-popsters Talking Heads. Today, R&B movers continue to flock to Sigma for its signature sound, even if things aren't quite what they used to be.

"These days anyone can make a great-sounding record all by themselves. As a result, recording is often more about building tracks than creative collaboration," says Tarsia, who left Sigma in 2003. "Progress is progress and nobody rides a horse to work any more – but the thing that music has lost is the energy and emotion that only occurs when you have a group of musicians playing together. I mean, when that rhythm section first locked on 'Didn't I (Blow Your Mind This Time),' the hair on my arms stood up. That just doesn't happen with one person and one machine."

914 STUDIOS
BLAUVELT, NY

After a fruitful decade in Manhattan, producer/engineer Brooks Arthur needed a change of scene. By the end of the 1960s a thriving artists' community had developed upstate, "and so I started to shop around for a piece of property in that direction," says Arthur. "Bearsville Studios was just getting started, people were starting to work outside of the city. I found this spot in Blauvelt, about 45 minutes north of Manhattan, which became 914 Studios. It was a nice solid brick building – a room within a room. It had a football field right outside where we'd have pick-up games between sessions; the Blauvelt Diner was right next door. It was a great location."

Fate intervened when, in May 1972, crooner/songwriter Paul Anka abruptly cancelled a week-long booking. "At the same time I got a call from Mike Appel, who was managing this guy from New Jersey named Bruce Springsteen. They wanted a flat rate to come in and start tracking Bruce's first album, *Greetings From Asbury Park*. The next thing I knew, Bruce was in my studio making records."

The following summer Springsteen was back in Blauvelt, where he took eight weeks to record his follow-up, *The Wild, the Innocent & The E Street Shuffle*. "He'd show up in this old VW bus," recalls Arthur. "There was a Carvel's right across the street; my daughters and Bruce would get ice cream together every day."

In 1974, with rock critic-turned-producer/confidante Jon Landau aboard, Springsteen made preparations to begin his next Columbia effort at New York's Record Plant, but not before cutting one last track at Arthur's place.

"One day I was playing my guitar on the edge of my bed, working on some song ideas, and the words 'born to run' came into my head," Springsteen later recalled. "At first I thought it was the name of a movie or something I'd seen on a car spinning around the Circuit, but I couldn't be certain. I liked the phrase because it suggested a cinematic drama I thought would work with the music I was hearing in my head."

Before entering the studio, Springsteen and the E Street Band spent months on the road working out a basic arrangement for 'Born to Run.' "But live, the limitations of a seven piece band were never going to provide me with the range of sound I needed to realize the song's potential," said Springsteen. "It became the first piece of music I wrote and conceived as a studio production. It was a turning point, and it allowed me to open up my music to a far larger audience." A key ingredient in 'Born to Run' was Arthur's so-called 'prepared piano,' slightly detuned to Bruce's specifications. "We used a bit of Eventide on the piano as well," recalls Arthur. "We also had this AKG spring echo unit, which Bruce loved – so much so that we began referring to it as the 'Spring-steen.'

"I like to think that Bruce was born at 914," says Arthur. "Years later I ran into Bruce, he came over and gave me a big hug. He said, 'You know the Blauvelt Diner? That was the last place I could get a breakfast and read the paper!'"

BEARSVILLE STUDIOS
BEARSVILLE, NY

Built by artist manager Albert B. Grossman in 1970, Bearsville Studios quickly gained favor among artists looking for an escape from the congestion of mid-town Manhattan. Situated in the Catskill Mountains region just two hours north of the city, Bearsville offered all the amenities of a full-service New York studio in a relaxing, rural environment. Bucking the smaller-is-better trend, today Bearsville's mammoth Studio A (60 by 40 by 38 feet) serves as a testament to the golden age of ambience. Studer tape machines, EMT plate reverbs and a pair of live chambers have allowed visitors like R.E.M., Phish, Todd Rundgren and Ozzy Osbourne to achieve a classic sound.

VAN GELDER RECORDING STUDIO
ENGLEWOOD CLIFFS, NJ

While working as an optometrist during the early 1950s, Rudy Van Gelder began moonlighting as a recording engineer, using his tiny living-room in Hackensack to bring the sounds of New York jazz to the world at large. Like most enterprising independents, Van Gelder hand-built his earliest console from spare radio-station parts. His mic collection was modest and he used effects sparingly. The details of his recording formula have remained closely guarded – Van Gelder went so far as to change mic positions when the groups were being photographed – but by keeping the players separated while encouraging leakage, Van Gelder was able to combine the intimacy of direct recording with the ambience of a full-on live performance.

Today, Van Gelder's Blue Note sides rank among the finest recordings in all of popular music. At the height of New York's 1950s and 1960s jazz movement, scores of major artists crossed the George Washington Bridge to record with Van Gelder, among them Miles Davis, Thelonious Monk, Eric Dolphy, and Coleman Hawkins.

Over a three-month period during 1957 and 1958, John Coltrane cut his stand-out *Lush Life* at Van Gelder's residence. Later called "the greatest jazz record ever made" by *Esquire*, Trane's *Lush Life* remains Van Gelder's personal favorite. "Things fell very well into place," notes Van Gelder, who built a permanent facility in nearby Englewood Cliffs a year later. "One of the things about Coltrane was that when it was done right, he knew it."

index

acknowledgements

PICTURE CREDITS The photographs reproduced in this book and on the jacket are almost all from Michael Ochs Archives/Redfern's, except: p.22/23 Frank Laico; p.152/153 New Eyes/Redfern's; and p.164/165 Photos By 'PoPsie' © 2004 Michael Randolph.

THE AUTHOR would like to thank the following for their participation and patience: Brooks Arthur; Randy Bachman; Tony Bennett; Hal Blaine; Artie Butler; Alice Cooper; Jason Corsaro; Marshall Crenshaw; Dennis Diken; John Einarson; Matthew Goldman; Lou Gonzalez; Al Gorgoni; Roy Halee; Jerry Harrison; Chris Huston; Janis Ian; Jimmy Johnson; George Klabin; Al Kooper; Frank Laico; Gene Lees; Jeffrey Lesser; Peter Lewis; Sherry Lookofsky; James Lowe; Bob Ludwig; Richard Lush; Arif Mardin; Robert Margouleff; Elliot Mazer; Mitch Miller; Don Puluse; Phil Ramone; Jim Reeves; Mike Rosenberg; Stan Ross; David Rubinson; Todd Rundgren; Walter Sear; Ed Stasium; Stephen Stills; Gordon Stoker; Joe Tarsia; Creed Taylor; Ken Townsend; Matt Wallace; Jerry Wexler; and Zal Yanovsky (the late great).

SOURCES The vast majority of quotes in this book are from interviews by the author, with the following exceptions. Jerry Wexler describing Tom Dowd comes from Wexler's autobiography with David Ritz, *Rhythm and the Blues* (Random House 1993). The Dowd quotes not attributed to Blair Jackson are from the documentary *The Language of Music*. The 'Shadow' Morton quote in reference to Artie Butler comes from a *Goldmine* interview by Richard Arfin published in 1991. The John Simon quote is from an interview with Lee Gabites at http://theband.hiof.no/articles/the_truth.html. The

Shelly Yakus quotes are from a ProSoundWeb online article by Bruce Borgerson at www.prosoundweb.com/recording/bruce_borgerson/shelly/shelly.shtml. And the Milt Gabler quote about the Pythian Temple is from Ted Fox's *In the Groove* (St Martin's 1986).

OTHER MATERIALS absorbed during research include a number of books: *Girl Groups: The Story of a Sound* by Alan Betrock (Bookthrift 1985); *The Beatles: Recording Sessions* by Mark Lewisohn (Harmony 1990); *For What It's Worth: The Story of Buffalo Springfield* by John Einarson & Richie Furay (Cooper Square 2004); *Shakey: Neil Young's Biography* by Jimmy McDonough (Random House 2002); and *Kind of Blue: The Making of the Miles Davis Masterpiece* by Ashley Kahn & Jimmy Cobb (Da Capo 2001). Some TV/film documentaries: the A&E Biography program *Brian Wilson*; *Tom Dowd & the Language of Music*; *Hitmakers: The Teens Who Stole Pop Music*; and *Inside Pop: The Rock Revolution*. Some periodicals: *Home Recording Magazine*; *Mix Magazine*; and *Goldmine* magazine. And a couple of prime websites: Spectropop.com; and ProSoundWeb.com.

THE PUBLISHER would like to thank: Paul Cooper; Kim Devlin; John Morrish; and Julian Ridgway.

"Making records used to be like painting. Then it turned into assembling."
Frank Laico.